African Plenty

African Plenty

A missionary life of miracles

Fred Ramsbottom
with David Lee

Marshall Pickering

Marshall Morgan Scott
Marshall Pickering
3 Beggarwood Lane, Basingstoke, Hants RG23 7LP, UK

First published in 1987 by Marshall Morgan and Scott
Publications Ltd
Part of the Marshall Pickering Holdings Group
A subsidiary of the Zondervan Corporation

British Library Cataloguing in Publication Data

Ramsbottom, Fred
African plenty.
1. Missions —— Africa
I. Missions II. Lee, David
266'.0092'4 BV3500

ISBN 0-551-01431-8

Phototypeset in Linotron Plantin by Input Typesetting Ltd,
London SW19 8DR
Printed in Great Britain by Anchor Brendon Ltd, Tiptree,
Essex

Contents

Introduction

In the late twenties the Congo — what is now called Zaire — was mostly uncharted wilderness. In the great colonial carve-up of Africa it had landed on the plate of the Belgians, who managed it as best they could with garrisons and government posts, and called it a dominion. But ruling a place like that from Europe was fraught with problems. It was so vast: if you'd been able to cut them up with scissors the forests and plains of the Congo would have made seventy Belgiums, or eight Britains with enough left over to duplicate most of the West Indies. Worse than that, it was unknown. Away from the coast and the few railways, the white man's strongholds were pinpricks on an empty map. Who shared this wasteland with the elephants and crocodiles and mosquito swarms no one really knew. In the places where a traveller smelled the distinctive odour of roasting human flesh, no one was keen to find out.

Away from the larger settlements, then, the Congo remained as it had always been, a land of mile-wide rivers, dense forest and savannas, of primitive squalor and spiritual darkness. Most of it seemed to have little commercial potential — you certainly wouldn't have gone there for a holiday — and that its remoter regions were opened up at all is owing in large measure to Christian evangelists, many of them sent by the Congo Evangelistic Mission (CEM). The founding of this organization was the life's work of two remarkable men — a cobbler, James Salter and a sea captain's son WFP

Burton. Once called by God they gave heart and soul to the work of evangelizing the Congo. Thomas Myerscough, pastor of the Pentecostal church at Preston, remained in Britain as Home Director, while Burton took charge of the Field overseas. The work grew, and as in Europe the Depression gave way to the unrest of the thirties God called others to join them. Few of these men and women knew what they were letting themselves in for by offering to pioneer for the gospel in a place like that. For a long time one of them didn't even know it existed, and wouldn't have thought twice about it if he had . . .

1: A night on the town

At eighteen I had just one problem, and his name was Foster Catterall.

Pulling my overcoat tight around me I looked up and down the empty street, then leaned over the parapet of Haslingden's only bridge. Reflections of the new street lights danced on the water.

It wasn't that life had given me an easy ride — far from it. I'd learned what work was about as a child when my father's health broke down under the strain of driving horses, day after day, the twenty-six miles into Manchester, carrying cloth for the textile merchants. It was a swift end to a short childhood. Suddenly I was out helping my mother on the poultry farm or earning a few extra pennies doing odd jobs for the farmer down the road. When the Depression came even my schooling went to the wall: instead like many other boys of my age, I made a weary trek across the countryside looking for work. I ended up apprenticed to an old man who repaired stone walls, but finally, and disastrously, came the General Strike. No work, no food, no coal. Every day, I seemed to be up on the moors behind the house digging peat, laying the blocks out to dry, then dragging them down to our house in the town to stave off the cold. But hardship hadn't broken my spirit. On the contrary, reaching manhood with that struggle behind me made me determined to enjoy life to the full. I had taken the worst that life could throw at me and I'd survived. Now, I felt, I was owed some sort of recompense, and if no one else gave it to me I'd go out and get it for myself.

Rehearsing my life story like this gave me a sense of soaring self-confidence that only faltered when I thought of Foster. I pulled a small piece of loose cement from the parapet and tossed it into the dancing lights below. Almost at the same moment they jerked up violently and I found myself overbalanced and staring down into a shadowy abyss.

'Watch out, Fred!'

It was Joe Lamb's voice; he had his full weight against me and my left arm twisted over the small of my back.

'Get off, you idiot! What are you trying to do?'

'Keeping you from fallin' in, Fred.'

'Like the blazes you are. Let me go!'

'Don't be ungrateful. I just saved your life.'

I growled at him, wrenched myself free and shoved him away with my foot. He landed on the seat of his pants in the street, laughing.

'That's the last time I 'elp you.'

'Next time I want your help I'll ask f'r it. Look at my shirt!'

'Look at his shirt!' mimicked Joe. 'Look at his shirt!'

'Do something with him, Maurice!'

'Oh-oh, taking sides now, are we? Come by me, Albert. Two against two's fair game.' Joe was scrambling to his feet; for a moment we confronted one another like wrestlers, ready to grapple.

'Come on, 'en.'

'We're ready for you. Ay, Maurice? Maurice!'

But Maurice had straightened. 'What are we fighting about?'

'My shirt. We're fighting about my shirt!'

'It's not even dirty.'

'You're just soft. If you don't want to help me, keep out of it.'

I grabbed Joe by the lapels and ran him against the lamp post, but the others pulled me off.

'All right, Fred, we know who's boss. Leave him be.'

Joe dusted himself down.

'So what are we going to do?'

We stood for a while, hands in pockets, and finally decided on the theatre where something called *A Musical Entertainment* was beginning. Eight flights of steps brought us to the balcony which locals called 'the gods'. This afforded a poor view of the stage but a good one of the audience, who were sitting in polite silence as a thin woman in dark green chiffon serenaded them from a grand piano. 'Oh . . . maybe it's because I'm a Londoner,' she sang in a voice as thin as her figure, 'that I love London so!' We applauded her vigorously if not sincerely. Joe whistled, the rest of us beat the rail with our fists and yelled, 'More, more!' People in the grand circle below glanced into the darkness behind them. By this time a small balding man in an evening suit had taken the stage to announce a Mr (the incredible Mr) Lori Fusi, famous conjuror from Naples. 'Hey! Bring back the lady!' cried Joe, but Mr Lori Fusi duly appeared, doffed his hat, and produced from it a white rabbit. Gentle applause from the stalls was backed up by raucous cheering from the gods. He reached into his breast pocket and with a great flourish pulled out not a handkerchief but two white rats. More cheering. His pockets were probably stuffed with mice but we never found out because at that moment light flooded on to our seats and we turned to see, awesomely silhouetted in the exit door, a pair of large, no-nonsense ushers.

Thrown out on the street we set about creating as much havoc as we could. For the whole two miles back to Haslingden we sang at the top of our voices, then raced down the streets banging on doors and running sticks along railings until people were opening their upstairs windows and yelling at us to keep quiet. That lasted about ten minutes, and then we gathered, breathless and more bored than we would admit, at the back of the pub. Maurice was first to let the side down.

'I'm off home.'

'Home? Now?'

'It's past midnight, Fred. I've to be up at six in the morning.'

'I've got to be back an' all,' said Albert, slouching away. 'See you tomorrow night, lads.'

We jeered at them, but it was getting colder and a couple of minutes later Joe and I split up and I made my way back down the lane to my parents' farm.

The anxiety returned now that I was alone again. Under a quarter moon I ran a few steps and punted a stone as hard as I could: it ricocheted from a fence, stuttered on the gravel and stopped. There was no getting away from it — Foster Catterall had forced me to see weaknesses in myself I would never have admitted. All his talk about God. Who on earth wanted God snooping around when they could look after themselves? It was ridiculous, I told myself. It had to be ridiculous. And yet, when I really thought about it, the things that I said were bringing me happiness — working like a demon and having a good time — always left me dissatisfied. I had the uneasy feeling there could be something more to being alive than I had so far discovered.

I could trace this uneasiness back to a nearly fatal accident at the local cinema. I'd taken an evening job there helping in the projection room, and had often done weekend work for the projectionist who, being an electrician, supplemented his income by installing electrical wiring. On this particular night, though, the projectionist didn't show up. It had been pouring with rain, and I was sitting in my damp clothes when I saw the manager's face appear in the little square of glass in the door. I opened it a crack.

'Start it up!' he hissed.

'What?'

'The projector!'

I glanced over my shoulder at the great machine that looked like a cross between a stage light and a maxim gun.

'You do know how to operate it?' the manager said, with a touch of sarcastic irritation in his voice. I nodded.

'Then get on with it. We're late!'

The door clicked shut. Actually I hadn't the faintest idea how to operate it — the projectionist had never shown me. But it seemed a splendid opportunity to show my mettle, so I laid both hands on the power lever the projectionist threw to start the generator below, and pulled. I felt a huge fist punch me in the chest. The projector, the light, the door — everything in the room — jerked forward, and I landed sprawling in a pile of empty spool cases three or four yards back from where I'd been standing. Water, I learned, was a very good conductor of electricity — I'd been lucky to escape with my life.

It was soon after this unpleasant little lesson that I first met Foster Catterall. He'd been put alongside me at the mill, and had a job like mine at another cinema in town. But although we had a lot in common we didn't get on — that is to say, *I* didn't get along with *him*. In fact being so often and so long in Foster's presence was torment because he was a keen Christian and persistently asked me if I was 'saved'. I didn't take kindly to it.

'Foster, will you please stop spouting about Jesus?'

But he would grin at me. 'I can't, Fred. He's so marvellous.'

'I *don't want* to *hear* about him.'

'Nor did I 'til last year. Fred, you have t' believe me — '

'I don't have to believe anyone. Let me live my own life. I'm getting on perfectly well without any help from God!'

'Don't you know in your heart that you need to be set free of your sins?'

At that point I would usually swear or turn my back on him. But try as I might I couldn't stop his questions getting to me. He'd challenge me at the mill and in return I'd tell him to shut up or ridicule him in front of my friends. Yet next morning as I got out of bed there was the same question sitting obstinately in my head, waiting to be answered. So I stepped up my activities. I went to a gymnasium, became a lightweight boxer and a proficient performer on the horizontal bars and rings. I got more aggressive and cynical; I proved myself with feats of daring, like climbing a factory chimney on ladders left by the steeplejacks. But in the end, after all the exertion and excitement, after yelling in the theatre and rioting in the streets — after all that, on my own again I was plagued by Foster's God and the fact that deep down I needed him.

'Fred, when are you going to get right with God and give your life to him?'

I spun round in the dark lane. That was Foster's voice! Sure enough out of the shadows emerged Foster Catterall, his footsteps turning quietly on the gravel. I realized then that I'd stopped. I was standing like a straw target, the words embedded hard and deep as arrows, and here was Foster coming to read his score. I turned on my heel and ran, but even as I did it I knew that running was pointless. It was a peculiar sensation to be young and strong enough to run five miles, and yet, after a few hundred yards, to be brought to my knees. My legs just crumpled beneath me, as though someone were loading logs on my back. And all I could hear in this still, calm night was: 'When, Fred? When are you going to give me your life?'

'Now,' I said. 'Now, Lord, now.'

2: *Opening moves*

For a moment Foster's jaw hung open, then he shut it and his customary grin reappeared.

'But Fred, that's wonderful! That's really wonderful!'

'It was just after you spoke to me.'

'And you gave your heart to the Lord there and then?'

'You can't think how good I feel!'

Men were pushing past us on their way up through the factory gates. Foster laid a hand on my shoulder. 'Come on. Follow me, and we'll find somewhere quiet.'

In the mill's spinning-room the great steam-driven mules were slamming noisily. We hurried past them, up by the side of the devilling machine that shredded the waste cloth, and scrambled up three flights of stairs into a long room full of cotton bales and shoddy. Here the deafening noise of the factory floor was reduced to a dull thud. 'Where are we?' I said.

'It's called the waste hole,' said Foster. 'This is where they store the raw stuff before it comes down to us on the machines.'

'It must be the only quiet room in the building.'

'Ay, it is.'

'You been here before?'

'Sometimes. It's a good place to pray before work.'

Looking at Foster I realized what my conversion had cost him. Those days I spent mocking him in front of our workmates had begun up here with him on his knees before God, praying for me.

'How do you pray?' I said.

'I give thanks to the Lord, and then I ask him for strength to remain true in my witness during the day, and to save the men I work with.'

'Like me, you mean.'

He smiled. 'We could meet up here every day if you want. I'd like the company.' 'Yes, so would I.'

In a brief pause we listened to the harsh metallic braying of the machinery. 'Foster — why did you decide to pray for me?'

'We work on the same mule together. Apart from that, I suppose I thought you were the sort of man God might touch.'

'Can I pray for someone?'

'Of course. Anyone you like.'

I closed my eyes and thought of the mild-mannered Maurice I'd envied and respected as long as I'd known him. 'Maurice Hugo, I want Maurice Hugo to be saved.'

Taking a leaf out of Foster's book I decided to set about helping God answer the prayer. When I arrived at the Hugos' home a couple of nights later they were finishing their tea. Maurice's father, a genial Cornishman, grasped my hand warmly and invited me in. He knew very well what a hot-head I was and had never let that stand in the way of his welcome, but even he took a second look when I announced the good news. They listened to my garbled version of the gospel amazed, not so much at what I was saying but that I of all people should be saying it. When he found a gap long enough to intervene Mr Hugo tapped his pipe on the hearth and said, 'Well, I don't know, young Fred. Something's happened to you, for sure.' It was to be a while before the same thing happened to him but Maurice, who had listened in his usual quiet way, gave his life to the Lord the next Sunday.

I was overjoyed. Being saved myself was exciting enough; setting out on the Christian way with a friend, promised to be a marvellous adventure. Of course there was a lot of catching up to do, and we began reading the Bible as a pair of starving men might devour a plate of food. As to finding a church, after a few weeks of exploration we settled on the Haslingden Town Mission, a plain little hall with a platform and chairs, where scripture was expounded faithfully by a pastor from the Holiness Movement. We found plenty of scope for service here. On the strength of five years' piano lessons I was immediately put to play the organ, and after a while when it became clear that the pastor's growing family would stretch his stipend too far, Maurice and I volunteered to save a caretaker's wages by cleaning the hall ourselves. More important, we were encouraged in our efforts to witness.

On a Saturday night we would take a group down to the market and spend an hour singing, shouting gospel texts, and pressing tracts into the hands of people whose attitudes varied from indifference to open hostility. In Charles Lane, the main access road to the mill, the reception was, if anything, slightly worse. At the market most of the crowd were strangers; but at work I was among men who had known me as I was — a foul-mouthed, rebellious youth. My only consolations were that in the end a couple of my workmates came to the Lord and that the rest, though they jeered and made threats, at least didn't pelt me with rotten fruit as occasionally happened at the market. At times like those it was sheer spirit and determination that kept me going.

I turned up at the Mission Hall one evening for my stint of cleaning after a particularly harrowing day in the Lane. Maurice and I had got into the habit of sitting down together at the start to pray and read the Bible, and this time we happened to fall upon the First Epistle to the Corinthians.

' "The manifestation of the Spirit is given to every man to profit withal," ' I read out loud.

' "For to one is given by the Spirit the word of

wisdom . . . to another the working of miracles; to another prophecy; to another discerning of spirits; to another divers kinds of tongues; to another the interpretation of tongues." '

'What on earth does that mean?'

Maurice shook his head, still scanning the verses. 'Beats me. What are tongues, and prophecy?'

'Have you ever heard anyone in our church prophesy?'

'I don't think so.'

'Then why does it say the manifestation is given to *every man?*'

'Maybe people here all have the same gift — faith or something.'

'But . . .'. We frowned at one another. 'Doesn't this say there should be somebody in the church with a gift of healing, somebody else with a gift of miracles?'

'That's what it seems to say.'

'We'll ask the pastor on Sunday.'

But on Sunday the pastor looked slightly alarmed and changed the subject.

Not long after we were attending one of the weekly Tuesday night prayer meetings at the mission hall when two newcomers arrived; a middle-aged woman and a girl with bright eyes and curly hair who looked to be about the same age as Maurice and myself. They sat down on the opposite side of the hall, and the meeting proceeded in its familiar fashion with a string of clear, sound and grammatical prayers. Then something very out of the ordinary happened. The girl began to pray; but as she prayed the words became weightless, as though they were carried by the Spirit himself and not on a human voice. This was prayer and praise as I had never heard it before, and there was more to come, for instead of finishing with an *Amen* the prayer receded slowly in another language, as if the girl were now saying what could be shared only between herself and God. Maurice and I exchanged glances. As soon as the meeting closed we raced over to introduce ourselves.

'Pleased to meet you,' she said, beaming. 'I'm Isabel Campbell. This is my mother.'

We shook hands politely.

'We haven't seen you here before.'

'That's because we haven't been, have we, Mum?'

'Are you going to join the church?'

She laughed. 'That depends on how the Lord leads. He brought us here tonight . . .'

It seemed an extraordinary thought, for God to lead you somewhere. 'I couldn't help noticing the way you prayed,' I said. 'Wanted to ask you . . .' Suddenly I felt as though I should be lowering my voice. 'What have you got that makes you able to pray like that?'

But she wasn't ashamed. 'I've been filled with the Holy Spirit,' she said.

'Filled?'

'When you're filled with the Holy Spirit he lets you pray in other tongues.'

'Is that what you were doing tonight, praying in tongues?'

'Of course. You didn't think I was speaking in French or something, did you?'

'But how did you get it? Can you stay a few minutes to tell us?'

Mrs Campbell nodded. It turned out that they worshipped at the Pentecostal Assembly in Blackburn, a Pentecostal Assembly being a place where everybody was filled with the Spirit and everybody prayed with the same spiritual power as Isabel. I could hardly imagine it. She also told us that God had called her to the Congo, a large country in Africa where hardly anyone knew of the Lord Jesus. I could hardly imagine that, either. I asked if it might be possible for Maurice and me to visit the Assembly in Blackburn.

'Why not next Sunday!' said Isabel.

Entering the Pentecostal church was like plunging into a hot bath after a dip in the sea. What struck me most strongly, apart from the warmth and spontaneity of praise, was that whereas in a Mission church everything was done by the pastor, here the service was carried along by the congregation. It was like the chapter we'd read in First Corinthians about different gifts being given to different people. Maurice and I absolutely revelled in it, and when I heard there was to be a baptismal service at a nearby Assembly in Burnley I hurried to put my name down on the list of candidates. Going down into the water that day it was as if I were being washed perfectly clean and filled with a glorious power exceeding all I had so far experienced. I was lost in praise and speaking the language of heaven. I learned afterwards that I'd come up with my face radiant. It was simply glorious, and I was walking around in a sort of holy haze for days.

Unfortunately the pastor at the Mission church didn't see it that way at all.

'I've called you three in here,' he said, bowed over his desk and clasping his fist, 'on account of this so-called doctrine of the Baptism of the Spirit. I'm sorry to have to say this. You, Fred, and Maurice, you have served the Lord faithfully here in our church. But it is my responsibility to tell you this teaching you have espoused is a dangerous falsehood.'

'But Pastor, being filled with the Spirit has completely changed us.'

'You may *think* it has changed you.'

'My prayer, my witnessing, everything has become so much more powerful since I went to the Assembly.'

'Fred, these are just feelings, nothing more.'

'The Baptism is taught in the Bible . . .'

'It's of the devil!' he snapped. 'Prophecy, tongues, it's all of the devil. Don't you understand that?'

'I can't reject something I know in my heart comes

from the Lord. And you can't deny, the gifts of the Spirit are talked about in the New Testament. Isn't that true?'

The pastor took a deep breath and addressed himself to Isabel. 'And you, Miss Campbell, you say you want to go to the Congo?'

'That's right, Pastor.'

'And you will not renounce this pentecostal heresy?'

'No, I will not.'

'Then I must tell you that you are as close to the Congo as you will ever get.' She made to reply, but he broke in, 'It's as clear cut as that. I'm sorry. You all of you face the same choice. You may renounce this doctrine and stay in this church, and no doubt in his own good time the Lord will advance you to the mission field or wherever he wishes you to go. If, on the other hand, you persist in preaching this devil-made falsehood I have no choice but to ask you to leave. Now which will it be?'

It was a sad choice, but a simple one.

3: *What happened in the Band Room*

We started attending the Assemblies in Blackburn and Burnley. There was a lot to do. Stephen Jeffries was then crusading in the area and he needed support and organization for his meetings. I found myself travelling up and down the Rossendale Valley giving help wherever it was needed, which as often as not meant heaving paralytics on to the platform to be prayed for. This was an education in itself; but I applied myself with no less dedication to studying the Bible. Every Tuesday night, whatever the weather, I would cycle the nine miles over the moors to hear the word expounded by Brother Watson at Blackburn Assembly; and as if that were not enough to be doing on top of a full-time job and extensive commitment to the church, I joined Maurice and Isabel in a correspondence course under the direction of Howard and John Carter at the Hampstead Bible Training School. Gradually, with my increasing knowledge of the Bible and long talks to Isabel about her calling to the Congo, I began to sense a plan for my life.

But the vocation was to begin a good deal nearer home than the Congo. It soon became clear to us that before we went much further in evangelizing the Rossendale Valley we should set up an Assembly in our own town of Haslingden. Almost unbelievably we stumbled on the perfect venue, only to find next day that we'd been beaten to it by — of all people — the Haslingden Brass Band. We thought hard.

'Where did the band meet before?' said Isabel.

'Down in Coal Hey, wasn't it? What does it matter?'

'Why don't we use the room they've left?'

Going to see it we discovered why the band had been so keen to leave. Two flights of stairs brought us into a large attic room where the windows had been bricked in and the only light filtered down through a couple of tiny grey skylights. As Maurice pointed out, it was less an Upper Room than a passable mock-up of the Black Hole of Calcutta. Clearly Haslingden Brass Band didn't want to be heard during practice.

Whether even this place could become Haslingden's first pentecostal Assembly still depended on the agreement of its owner, and since she was known as a staunch Roman Catholic our chances seemed pretty slim. I was delegated to see her, and made my way to her impressive home on Townsend Street. An enormous man answered the door.

'She's out,' he said in answer to my enquiry.

'Should I come back later?'

'What do you want?'

'I believe she owns a room over three houses in Coal Hey, where the band used to meet. I'd like to rent it.'

He raised his eyebrows. 'Then I suppose you'd better come in.' I stepped into a carpeted hall with ornate cornices and gold-framed mirror fixed above a polished table. 'Come far, have you?'

'Just the other side of town.'

'I seem to remember seeing you . . .'

I wondered how good a shot he was with a tomato.

'I'm down at the market on Saturday evenings quite a lot.'

'Don't think it was there. Sell something, do you?'

'No, I go with some friends of mine to . . . preach the gospel.'

'Really?'

'We belong to the Assembly in Blackburn.'

'Well, well. I haven't been into church for years. Of course I'm a Catholic . . .'.

The extraordinary thing was, I got along with this man like a house on fire. He didn't resent in the least my telling him how I'd been saved and filled with the Holy Spirit: he kept on asking me to tell him more, and when his sister came home he insisted that I go through the whole story again and didn't hesitate to expand on some point I was glossing over.

But of course sooner or later we had to come down to brass tacks.

'For a Pentecostal Assembly?' she said carefully. 'I shall have to think about this . . .'.

No doubt she was thinking also about the neighbours, and her confessor. The two of them conversed in low voices by the French windows, leaving me seated by the hearth trying to catch snippets of their discussion. 'Dreadful state . . .' ' . . . really think they can . . .' ' . . . wouldn't like to think . . .'. Then the brother said quite loudly, 'In that case we should give it to them right away, this week.'

I almost dropped through the floor. Even half an hour later when I left the house on Townsend Street with the contract and rent book in my hand I could hardly believe the room was mine. Against all the odds Haslingden Assembly was under way.

But we had our work cut out transforming the old band room into a church. For one thing, nobody would be able to read a hymn book in there until the windows were replaced, and that meant moving bricks three storeys up on the outside of the building. Since our best ladder reached only the middle of the second, it took two strong men standing on a piggy-back and an arrangement of tables to get me high enough for the job. Similar makeshift scaffolding had to be rigged up inside to paint the ceiling, and I am glad to say that we all survived, though looking back on it I can't imagine how.

The entire redecoration was done without our having more than a few pennies to rub together. In the tradition of the time, whatever money we earned was handed over to our respective parents in exchange for our keep and a little pocket money. Whatever materials we required therefore had to be obtained by faith in God's provision. So too did the specialist skills needed to use them. None of us had much experience of plastering or painting or fitting windows, but with a lot of effort, perseverance and prayer we arrived at that happy juncture in the work when all the major jobs were done and it remained only to clean up and fill the place with furniture.

This was more easily said than done, as the number of people we expected for the opening service far exceeded the number of chairs we'd begged and borrowed to sit them on. It might also, I said privately to Maurice, exceed the strength of the floor to hold them up, since we hadn't been able to replace the rotten boards. As time wore on we grew steadily more anxious. With only one week to go we came to the conclusion that the marvellous success of the redecoration had made us proud, yet soon after we repented of that — lo and behold — what should appear in the local paper but an advertisement offering a large quantity of benches! When he heard what we wanted them for, the seller was willing to let them go for a nominal sum, and after carrying them laboriously up the two flights of stairs and laying them out in rows from front to back of the church we sat down and heaved a very big sigh of relief.

When it comes to catering for a crowd there is no greater asset than a mother, and since between us we had three, providing tea for the congregation proved relatively easy. We had planned two meetings for the first Saturday, one at three o'clock, one at seven; but long before the afternoon meeting people started to arrive and as the room filled up and visitors had to resort to boxes or lean against walls, an atmosphere of tingling expectancy gripped the new church. When we began the service with hymns of praise to God it was as if waves of the Holy Spirit were washing over us. The room seemed to shake with God's power. No one could preach a sermon because the worship didn't let up — everyone was singing and dancing together, and even the veterans like Thomas Myerscough and Fred Watson were being lifted and filled with the Spirit of God. In fact during the entire meeting only two people left: Maurice and I had crept behind the partition to pray for the floor.

As the Spirit swept along the Rossendale valley our Assembly was joined by three more. We saw numerous miracles and scores of people filled with the Holy Spirit. One healing happened to a member of our own congregation, which after the opening service stayed steady at about thirty-five members. This particular man had contracted acute pneumonia. The doctor said there was nothing to be done and the relatives began to gather at the house in anticipation of his death. Maurice and I were on our way to see him when we both received a sudden strong assurance from the Lord that our brother was going to be healed. Without that I think we might have been discouraged entering his room in the reverent silence that surrounds an impending death and seeing his pale, lined face. But when we laid our hands on him and prayed, almost immediately his colour returned. It was only a matter of days before he was back on his feet again and worshipping with us at the church.

Miracles of this sort constantly accompanied the preaching of the gospel during this revival. Maurice, Isabel and I also saw many members of our own families brought to the Lord, the first in mine being my second to youngest brother, Harry, who suddenly and to my great surprise decided that going week by week with the rest of the family to Salem Methodist Church didn't make him a Christian, and asked me what he should do. After that, one by one, the rest of my brothers and sisters followed.

One other important thing happened while we were at Haslingden Assembly: after three years of working and growing together in the Lord Isabel and I got married.

4: The call

It came on a perfectly ordinary day at the mill. I was standing across the mule from Foster, humming to myself as I watched the eight hundred spindles dispensing their yarn, when quite out of the blue the rhythmic motion of the machine seemed to turn into a sea of black faces. As I'd hardly even seen an African before the vision was doubly startling. All of them had their hands stretched out towards me and were crying, 'Come over and help us, or we shall die!' As I stood numbly taking this in I heard another voice, speaking this time from within my own heart. 'Fred, my servant,' it said, 'are you willing to leave all to go and tell them?' The crowd of Africans were still reaching out to me. 'Oh Lord,' I said, 'I will. I'll go wherever you want me to go . . .'

'Fred! Fred, are you all right?'

Suddenly I was looking at the mule again, its wide rows of yarn switching up and down, criss-crossing.

'Fred!' shouted Foster again from the other side of the machine.

'Yes, Yes I'm fine.'

I beckoned him over. 'Foster, I've just had a vision. God's calling me to Africa!'

The grin that had so infuriated me before my conversion spread all over Foster's face and he shook me by the shoulders. 'Praise God!' he shouted, barely audible over the clapping of the mule.

Really this vision was less a call in its own right than a confirmation of half-formed plans and long cherished hopes. Isabel, of course, had felt drawn to the Congo before the day we met, and as she shared this feeling with Maurice and me during our years at Haslingden Assembly, getting to the Congo as missionaries had become our common dream. From a practical point of view the Congo looked a poor choice if only because, on top of all the other preparations, we would have to learn French — the colonial language of the country. But we found a French teacher and committed ourselves solemnly to the task, which involved a weekly trip to Bolton and a lot of hard graft, eased only a little by Isabel, who was the only one of us who'd studied French at school.

The big problem apart from language study was finding a missionary organization willing to send us, so we were very excited to receive a visit from Teddy Hodgson on furlough from the Congo Evangelistic Mission. We must have spent half the night asking him questions about the work and being asked in return whether we were up to the grim challenges a country like the Congo could present. But when we finally went to bed Isabel and I felt disappointed: we had covered nearly every detail of church work in the Congo and yet for all that we had been given no positive guidance. Could it be we weren't being called there after all? As Teddy Hodgson came down stairs for breakfast next morning we waited in trepidation.

'Listen,' he said, bashing his egg sharply and reaching for the salt, as though his advice was insignificant enough to be deferred, 'I've been praying over night and I think you should go along and see' (he took a mouthful of egg and chewed it) 'Thomas Myerscough, our Home Secretary.'

'You think we might be able to go to the Congo?'

'That's not for me to say, but Tom will give you the forms.'

Actually Tom Myerscough wasn't as forthcoming with

the application papers as Teddy Hodgson had said. He knew us quite well by the time we took the train to Preston to see him — he had come to the opening service at Haslingden — but that didn't let us in for any special favours. He sat rocking slightly in his old leather chair as we told him about our calling to the Congo, and when we'd finished our story he simply said, 'Hmm,' his eyes fixed somewhere above our heads. 'And how many souls have you won for the Lord Jesus Christ?' he said finally.

We totted up hurriedly. 'About a dozen.'

'Marvellous, marvellous,' he said, rubbing his long beard lingeringly with both hands. 'Well then. Go back home, and when you have won as many again come back and see me.'

This was one eventuality we really hadn't bargained for. But beneath the awful feeling of deflation we had coming out of his office, there was a gritty determination to do what was required, and in a few months we were back in Preston once again.

Tom Myerscough listened quietly, as he had before. 'Marvellous,' he said, smiling. 'Marvellous. Now would you mind going away and winning twelve more . . . ?'

It began to dawn on us that in the Mission's view more was needed to make a missionary than simple zeal. Staying power and experience were vital qualities too and could only be built up by sticking to our work in Haslingden. By now I had given up my job at the mill to work full-time for the Assembly, and I redoubled my efforts to preach the gospel and bring new Christians into the church. They were certainly testing times. The joy of having Isabel give birth to our son Alan was balanced by pressure from our relatives to examine our call overseas in the light of our newly-acquired family responsibilities. On top of this, for three months Isabel and I were separated while she went to stay in France with Pastor Pierre Nicolle and his wife, leaving her mother and me to cope with a one year old and very bouncy baby. In the end I left Haslingden Assembly in Maurice's hands and went out to join her.

Acceptance by the Congo Evangelistic Mission hung on the results of our French examination, set in London in Easter of 1933. We took the boat back across the Channel still a good deal less than fluent, but trusting that if God wanted us out on the Mission Field He would get us through the exam. In London we met the other candidates: Jim Fowler, Leslie Wigglesworth (grandson of the famous Smith) who'd been studying in Belgium, and Alfred Brown of the Preston Assembly who had left Cliff College to evangelize in Newfoundland, Canada.

We were examined by a Mr Tilling, whose father, so Mr Tilling told us, had put his name on every bus in London by owning the city's first bus company. He himself had stepped off the footplate and gone into the Foreign Office. Besides being a consular official he was one of the pioneers of the British pentecostal movement, which was the reason CEM had selected him for the job of examiner. The ordeal was relatively painless: for a couple of hours he conversed with us as a group to test our familiarity with the spoken word, and at the end, to make sure we could write it as well, he asked us each to produce a short essay on a biblical character of our choice. I think I managed five hundred words on Joseph.

Much worse than the exam was the long wait to find out what had come of it. Isabel and I were only too well aware that failure at this point could put an end to our hopes of service in the Congo — in effect our ability to speak French was the litmus paper being used to detect our calling. When after several agonizing days the plain brown envelope bearing CEM's embossed initials fell through our letter box, neither of us wanted to open it. But it carried good tidings: not just we, but all five candidates had been accepted. In two months we would be on our way.

Hectic preparations ensued. We attended the Easter

Convention at Preston Assembly, the mother church of all the Assemblies in the North-West, to be presented to the congregation. James Salter, the new Home Director of CEM, took us down to London to arrange for passports and tickets, and as our departure date approached we set about packing such belongings as we could take on the journey, the cost of which was borne largely through the sacrificial giving of our own small Assembly at Haslingden.

On the Friday before we left we joined an enormous gathering for the valedictory service at the old Zion College in London. Many of the founder figures of CEM and the Assemblies of God were there — including the Salters, the Tillings and Smith Wigglesworth himself — as well as many friends from the churches we'd worked with in Rossendale. It was during this splendid send-off, when hands were laid on us and we were formally set apart for the work of God in Africa, that we felt our task as missionaries had really begun. On June 11th, 1934, we set sail from Tilbury on one of the last coal-burning steamers, the *Llanstephan Castle*, and made our way south down the west coast of Africa. Isabel and I were housed in the cabin Mr Salter had fought strenuously to avoid — the one over the propellers. The thudding of the engine reminded me of my days in the mill, though it was less regular and far quieter than the mules, and I would often lie awake at night thinking of Foster and the course of events he'd set in motion to bring me, finally, on this journey.

Leslie Wigglesworth was with me on deck when we caught our first sight of Lobito Bay in Angola. There wasn't much to see except a quay and some low sand-dunes.

'Do you know what it means — Lobito Bay?' I asked.

'Passage way.'

'That's appropriate.'

Leslie smiled. 'You could say that. It used to be a

slave port. For a lot of Africans I suppose this was the last sight they had of their home.'

In a couple of hours the five of us were standing alone on the quay watching the last little vestige of England pull away, dragging her lines after her.

5: *Into the real thing*

Riding into Central Africa on the Benguela Railway in 1934 wasn't exactly travelling in the lap of luxury. Our ascent to the Angolan desert was oppressively hot. The dust ploughed up by the locomotive would sweep in through the windows and cover everything in the compartment. It got into our packing cases and when we went to have our meals we found it served up in the food. But we cheerfully jumped down from the train every time it stopped at a wayside station to see whatever we could of the new continent. Often this was little enough, but at one such stop we picked up a Methodist Episcopalian Bishop by the name of John Springer, who whiled away the hours by giving us a lot of very good advice about missionary work in the Interior. After a day and a half the train crossed into the Belgian Congo finally depositing us at Tenke where we waited three days in a small Greek hotel until the next train arrived. From here on, the journey was through dense tropical forest. The engine, a wood-burner, belched out black smoke and sparks as it climbed on to the high plateau to Kabondo Dianda, a town with a mission station and military camp, which was as far as the railway went.

We were met by the incongruous sight of a crowd of singing Africans in traditional dress of brown raffia led by a Welshman, Garfield Vale. Their welcome, like their singing and their worship, was completely overwhelming. We were swept up along with our luggage and taken through the open woodland to the mission station, the only car available being used to carry Isabel and Alan. Just how different everything looked when you got to Africa was bewildering in the extreme. These Africans, who gestured and conversed in a way I couldn't begin to interpret, sang hymns to familiar tunes and did it more lustily than the best gospel choir in Britain. Streets that at home would have been crowded with cars were dirt tracks in the Congo, and such as there were had made strange adaptations to their new environment. (The van Harold and Josephine Womersley arrived in that first afternoon had been stripped of its body and reassembled, as I said to Isabel, like a flying bedstead.) Worst of all, and to my great embarrassment, nobody — not even the white missionaries — was wearing plus fours! Suddenly our whole lives had changed in a way our intensive preparations had not quite equipped us for. Nor did our colleagues in the Field encourage us to hesitate on the brink of this new way of life — our testimonies delivered on the first Sunday marked the last time we were allowed to use a European language in a local church.

'How are you getting along?' said Garfield Vale, joining me on the verandah of the mission station on our third day.

'Not too bad,' I said. 'It's all a bit of a shock.'

'You'll get over that.'

'How long did it take you to learn the language?'

'Kiluba? I learned very slowly at the start, but after a while I got the hang of it. It's really not that difficult when you've got the basics. The Baluba will be very willing to teach you.'

'Baluba?'

'That's what the people in this region are called.' He patted my shoulder. 'I came to tell you the Executive Council have decided where you're all going. Jim and Leslie will be heading north with the Womersleys, and

Alfred is to join Mr Burton at Mwanza. You have not met Mr Burton?'

'No, I haven't.'

'You won't forget it when you do. Once seen, never forgotten.'

'What about Isabel and myself?'

'You will be staying here with us — '

I felt a faint wave of relief.

' — which means among other things that you will need a house.'

'Does that mean we have to buy one?'

'No, it means you have to build one. Making bricks with the Baluba will help you learn their language. When you have enough bricks you can build a house. Until then we'll get the men to put together a shack for you. It won't be much, but it'll keep you dry until the house is finished.'

That night I wrestled with the most awful temptation. To be out here in the middle of Africa, far from all I recognized as home, to have to build my own house — even make the bricks to build it out of — when I had no skill as a craftsman, all this seemed miserable in comparison to the life I could have led in Britain. After all, it wasn't as if I hadn't been offered other jobs in the church, jobs with people I understood, jobs where I could speak in my own native tongue. How on earth was I going to last out in the Congo, bring up a family, preach the gospel, when I couldn't speak a word of the same language? The prospect left me completely drained. But then I remembered a verse of the Bible I had learned in my earliest days as a Christian: 'submit yourself to God, resist the devil and he will flee from you!' Somehow when I concentrated on that everything fell into its proper perspective. I wasn't here on my own accord; I had been called here by God, and if I faced temptations and hardships they were no more than I could cope with if I only stood firm and resisted. I lay in the darkness repeating the verse over and over until I fell asleep and awoke the next morning fresh for my first day at the anthills, digging earth for brick-making.

When I finished the house ten weeks later I was already able to pick out a few Kiluba words. My communication with the other workers, painful at first, had slowly gone beyond gestures and now included simple sentences, albeit rather clumsily delivered. The work itself had been interrupted occasionally by trips to surrounding villages with Garfield, to initiate me into the care of the young churches that in this period of revival were springing up on every side. He was a great missionary and a sound teacher. But as soon as we got back to the station I would be back at the building, spurred on not least by the thought of all the creeping insects awaiting us in our makeshift little hut. The prospect of living in a brick building once again was as precious to us as that of woollen underwear to a hermit in a hair shirt. We had only moved in for two weeks, however, when with the irritating way life has of depriving you of something you've spent a long time working for and not had time to enjoy, a letter arrived from Mr Burton informing us that we were to be moved 150 miles north-east to Kisanga, where William and Fanny Hall were long overdue for a furlough.

Garfield's parting gift to me was an unwelcome invitation to preach at the Sunday morning meeting in my jerry-built Kiluba. How I got through twenty minutes the Lord alone knows, but with many stammerings and pauses I managed to preach from John 4 about the woman at the well. At the time I must confess I felt little more than embarrassment, but on a trip to Kabondo Dianda four years later I learned that there had after all been a higher purpose in it, because an elderly man approached me and asked if I remembered the sermon. 'Yes,' I replied. 'It was about Jesus giving the woman the water of eternal life.' 'Exactly right!' he said to me.

On that day I gave my heart to Jesus, and I've been drinking from the eternal spring ever since!'

It took three days to repack our belongings in boxes small enough to be carried by hand. There was of course no railway to Kisanga, not even a road, so we faced the prospect of travelling for ten days over the harsh terrain of the bush, and being almost completely dependent on our African guides. A worse ordeal for a white family fresh from the comforts of Europe can hardly be imagined. Isabel and I went most of the way on bicycles (which the Baluba called *Nkinga*), while Alan was carried in a hammock slung on a long pole. Bringing up the rear in legendary fashion was a string of native bearers, each carrying a small part of our household. Though we didn't know it then, this once familiar arrangement of white man followed by load-bearing Africans was not a lame concession to white supremacy. The Africans let the white man go in front for the simple reason that the first man in line collected all the flies.

Though we asked the headman to rouse us as early as possible so we could travel in the coolest part of the day, it didn't take long for the sun to turn the land into an oven. Conscious of the need to make good time I always pressed on as far as I could before the heat compelled us to stop. On the edge of the savanna, where the only shelter available was beneath the occasional tree, 'pressing on' generally meant cycling on past one tree in the hope of finding another further on. I knew I'd gone too far when an exasperated voice behind me called out 'Don't bother looking for any more trees. I didn't really want to stop for lunch anyway!' We inevitably pulled up at the next one.

Lunch under a tree in the Congo is no picnic, and we soon learned that if you didn't want to share your sandwiches with the local insects there was nothing for it but to stand up. But this was a minor inconvenience in comparison to the mosquitoes that at dusk came out not just in ones and twos but by the battalion. Only two things would keep them at bay: fire, which we lit religiously as soon as darkness fell, and mosquito nets, rigged up over Alan's hammock pole leaving just enough room for our camp beds. We were to see a lot more of these dreadful creatures during our stay in the Congo, and had already started taking the daily dose of quinine which in those days was the only remedy for malaria. It came as a powder, and was so bitter that the only way you could stomach it was to roll it in a little ball of dough. This wasn't completely effective: taking too much or too little of it could leave you with the kidney failure known in Africa as blackwater fever. But as the alternative was a crippling and usually fatal dose of malaria there really wasn't any choice. Without quinine your chances of catching the disease were in the order of thousands to one, and it went without saying that your chances of avoiding a bite were virtually non-existent. I remember once wading through a swamp and feeling the insects landing on the back of my neck; when I slapped it with my hand and smeared them off, they left my palm bloody.

We finally arrived exhausted and saddle-sore in Kisanga to be greeted by the Halls, the nurse Bessie Swettenham, and a crowd of singing Africans among whom were fifty-two *Basapudi*, or native evangelists. In a sense, by coming to this little mission station where an older missionary couple had been working for a long time and had already built up a lively and thriving church, we were being let in the easy way. True, we were out on our own as far as European company was concerned, but there's a lot of difference between pushing a car that's already moving and starting one from a dead stop. But that might be to give the wrong impression. After all, nothing in the Congo was ever really *easy* . . .

6: *How to be ill in the Congo*

For the next six months, while Isabel took care of the Kisanga mission, I spent my time in almost continuous travel between the out-stations, staying in villages and learning the customs and language of the Baluba. The job was made a bit easier by a tall African carpenter called Fidipa, one of the *Basapudi*, who acted as guide and became a close friend.

I formed a lot of striking impressions of native life that never left me. For instance, the first thing you notice on entering an African village is the smell — the slightly fetid, animal smell of a place constantly lived in and rarely cleaned. It was usually worst in the huts, the mud-and-wattle structures with a grass thatch built in a square style borrowed from the Basongye people further north. Out on the savanna these huts would be fairly large and well spread out, but in the bush, where space was severely restricted by the trees, you might find two dozen huts crammed together in a clearing no bigger than a tennis court. In each one a smoky fire would be lit at night to keep the mosquitoes at bay.

The people themselves, who were very black, still wore traditional dress — a rough brown blanket tied at the waist and woven from the leaves of the raffia palm. I soon learned that clothing played an important part in the society of the village. A man's position could usually be judged from the number and type of beads he wore on his wrists or neck, the largest ones — a pure blue — being reserved for the headman. These beads, Mr Hall told me before he left, had originated in Arabia and reached the Congo by a long chain of trade. They were therefore highly valued and often used for bartering between tribes.

Another aspect of African life we could hardly fail to notice — since we shared it — was the food. Sweet potato and palm nuts became my staple diet on these trips in the bush. We also ate a lot of manioc, or cassava. The sort we ate roasted or boiled at the station, the Baluba called 'sweet' manioc, though it wasn't actually sweet to taste, just milder than the bitter variety they used. This preference was explained by the greater size of the root, and the fact that until you had soaked it for several days in a river pool and dried it in the sun, it was actually poisonous, and thus less likely to be stolen from the soil. In addition, something regarded as a great delicacy among the natives was the flying ant, so much so that on a day when the ants were taking to the air villagers would build fires to attract them. Once trapped and roasted the ants had the texture of burned toast, and to give them their due were extremely nourishing, though Isabel could never be induced to try one.

Living, travelling and talking with the Baluba I quickly got acquainted with the language, with the result that my preaching had greater impact. I felt that the six-month stint standing in for the Halls had given me a sound in-service training for whatever lay ahead, and by the time James Salter came to visit us on his way through to Kabongo I was all geared up for the next assignment. But he didn't say much about it, and after we had talked over dinner about the joys and difficulties of this first posting at Kisanga he took me aside. 'I'm concerned for Isabel,' he said quietly.

This took me by surprise. 'Isabel? Why?'

'It's not easy, you know, for the missionary wife.

You're the one who gets all the excitement; she has to stay at home and keep the station together, and do it practically single-handed. That's not easy.'

'We talked about it. We agreed — '

He touched my hand lightly. 'Yes, of course you did. I'm just saying, when you get out in the Field it's a lot harder than you expect. I think Isabel's looking tired. She could do with a rest. In fact you all could.'

'What do you suggest?'

'There's a station south of here; not far, at Kikondja. You'll know the man down there from England — he's Teddy Hodgson. He'll be delighted to look after you for a few weeks. If I were you I'd write to him and ask. In fact,' Mr Salter smiled, 'I'm going to make you do it right now.'

The holiday was swiftly arranged, and Isabel, Bessie and I prepared to march the thirty-eight miles in the same way we had come from Kabondo Dianda, carrying Alan in a hammock. But by now we were at the end of the wet season, the elephant grass was tall on the plains, the paths narrow and difficult, the sun oppressively hot. After six hours of walking we came to a river and decided to sit out the early afternoon. Any contact with river water in the tropics is dangerous, but with no villages visible upstream the chances of contracting hookworm were comparatively small, and because the sun was baking hot, we took our shoes off and dandled our feet in the water. It was icy cold.

The next day when we arrived at Kikondja Alan was flushed and fretful. 'What's the matter with him?' I said to Isabel, grasping the limp, too-warm hand between finger and thumb.

'I don't know, Fred. But it looks like something I had when I was sixteen — rheumatic fever.'

We consulted with Teddy Hodgson, who agreed that we should get back to Kisanga as quickly as possible. So, our ill-fated holiday over in a matter of hours, we returned home, with greater difficulty this time because of Alan's worsening condition and the chill Bessie had taken in her feet. Late on the second day we made it, and after a short night's sleep I set out with Fidipa to find Mr Burton, fifty miles east in Mwanza. It wasn't the way I had expected our first meeting to be. I found myself explaining things to him breathlessly as though I were passing on the baton in a relay, and no sooner had he got the gist of my story than he ran out to fetch the doctor from the nearby government post, giving me hasty directions to meet him at the crossroads in a couple of hours. It was with good cause the Africans had named him *Kapamu*, literally, 'the rusher-forth'.

When he came, however, he was slightly winded, and on his own.

'I'm sorry, Fred. Tried everything I could, but he's not going to come. He'll only treat Alan if you bring him here.'

'*What?*' I burst out.

But Mr Burton, who was a large man, waved a hand dismissively. 'No good arguing. It's policy, we have to live with it. Take Fidipa and get back here as soon as you can.'

The second journey to Mwanza was a nightmare. For a start we were carrying Alan in a litter, which slowed us up anyway, but on top of that the slightest jolt caused him awful pain in his joints, with the result that he cried out constantly and we lost time through taking care to be gentle. We had reached the tall grass and light woodland that Africans call the *Kiala* when Fidipa motioned me to stop. I thought he wanted to shift the weight of the litter. He was looking right and left into the towering grass.

'I smell fire.'

'You sure?'

We laid down the litter and strained to see over the grass. It was a gamble we had taken in making a rapid journey in the dry season, that no one between Kisanga and Mwanza was burning the grass to trap game. The practice was fantastically dangerous even for the hunters, because fire spread over the savanna as fast as a man could run and switched direction unpredictably with the wind. I'd heard stories of women following a fire to dig up snakes and rats, being caught as it turned. Missionaries I knew had brought them in still alive, their feet and calves burnt to charcoal.

'There!'

Fidipa was pointing above the tall grass behind us, where a grey haze was rising in the sky.

'Where's it going?'

'Like us — it is following the wind.'

We picked up the litter and ran clumsily for perhaps half a mile to a low ridge where the elephant grass was short enough to see over. Already small charred flakes were blowing around us like black snow. The fire, now audible, ran on a broad front, outflanking us on both sides. Alan began to wail.

'We need a firebreak.'

'How?'

'The wind's going across us where we are now. I reckon we've got about twenty minutes before that fire reaches us. If we can start our own fire, down by that tree, we may be able to burn out the land between and stop it getting here.'

Fidipa stayed with Alan while I made my way about two hundred yards down the slope, broke up some fine, dry grass for kindling and put a flame to it. It caught fast, crushing the tall grass under a wheel of flame. We picked up the litter, moved around behind and retreated slowly. In a matter of minutes the first fire was so close we could no longer distinguish it from our own. We seemed to be wedged between two twenty-foot walls of flame, close enough now for us to feel the heat on our flesh, making us gulp for breath. There was nothing we could do. We crouched over Alan's bed to protect him from the flying embers, and prayed. At that moment, as though one of the Seven Seals was being opened, we heard a loud trumpeting. We stared rigid and wide-eyed in the direction of the sound and felt the ground begin to shake. '*Nzuvu!*' cried Fidipa, 'Elephants!'

The panic-stricken herd was wheeling round against the fire and heading straight for us. I cannot describe the feeling you get when you know for a certainty that in a matter of seconds you are going to be trampled into pulp by wild elephants. It must have been something like what the Israelites felt on the shores of the Red Sea when they heard behind them the stampeding chariots of Pharoah. I remember clutching Alan to me and saying, or yelling, something like, 'Lord! Deliver us!'

They appeared over the grass, two massive bulls at the head. The blur of grey was the herd running blindly behind. Like a thundercloud they bore down on us until they were only ninety feet away, then — then, unbelievably, as though struck by Moses's staff, they divided. One bull turned off to our left, the other careered on past us to the right, and the herd sliced in two after them. Crouching on the ground in the middle it felt as though we were inches from a high speed train: there was a deafening confusion during which we huddled together with our eyes screwed tight closed, Then, a sudden quiet. I looked up to see the herd retreating over our firebreak, and gave thanks with my heart thudding inside my chest. Then I scrambled to my feet. 'That's our way out. Let's go after them.' And we picked up the litter and hurried away. Five hours later, and desperately tired, we stumbled into the Mwanza Mission.

'Well, how's my little chum?' said Mr Burton. 'Quite an adventure for you, eh?'

'Can we get to the doctor tonight?' I asked.

Mr Burton shook his head. 'The government post's another seven miles. They'll all be in bed by now, and it wouldn't be doing Alan a favour for you to set out again now. We'll just have to pray.'

This turned out to be very effective. On our way to the post next morning Alan suddenly started to sing his favourite hymn, 'Jesus, lover of my soul, let me to thy bosom fly . . .' The bearers laid the litter gently on the ground and began to praise God. 'He will not die, for the Lord has touched him,' they said. 'Have we not heard his voice again? He will live!' The doctor, who seemed slightly ashamed of himself for making us bring a sick child through a bush fire, bandaged Alan carefully and invited us to stay in his house overnight. The progress of Mr Burton's 'Little Chum' became such an important topic of local gossip that when he had recovered ten days later we weren't allowed to leave Mwanza without parading him, standing up in his hammock, the whole length of the village.

After failing so dismally in our attempt at a holiday we decided with Mr Salter's consent that the next best thing was at least to avoid another move, with the result that we stayed at Kisanga for another year. There was plenty to do, including an extension to Bessie Swettenham's house that required the moulding and kiln-baking of literally thousands of bricks. I set out on another series of tours, and finally organized a fortnight's training course at the mission station for all the teachers and evangelists working in the area. This took me back to the great pentecostal conventions I'd been to in north-east England. It was amazing how two weeks spent studying the scriptures equipped us all with fresh spiritual strength to return to the villages. But I wasn't to make any more preaching trips around Kisanga. Instead, in 1936 we were called down to see Mr Burton.

7: Cannibals and dried elephant

'. . . Things are changing, Fred. Hitler re-arming in the Rhineland, now Civil War in Spain. We're going to be in the middle of a scrap soon, I can see that.'

Looking out from Mr Burton's verandah over a green savanna that changed only with the seasons it was hard to imagine what he called a scrap affecting us here. I had never taken much interest in European politics, and I waited while he fanned himself with his hat and gazed into the distance. Eventually he pulled himself up in his chair.

'Still, that's on somebody else's plate for now. Fred, I called you down here because a new opportunity's come up and I thought you and Isabel might be interested.'

'Away from Kisanga?'

'At Katompe, about two hundred miles north. It's a new station, and it would be your job to open the area up. Nobody even knows where the villages are round there.'

'It sounds marvellous!'

'Well hang on a minute.' Smiling, he gently punched my arm. 'You won't find it a bed of roses. You're out of Baluba country there and into Basongye. That'll virtually mean learning another language.'

'We don't mind that.'

'No. Good. But I'm warning you now that this posting isn't just difficult — it could be very dangerous.'

'Why?'

'The Basongye aren't as accustomed to the white man as the Baluba are. You may find them hostile. You'll certainly be facing a lot of witchcraft and idol worship which will make your job as a missionary far tougher than it's been at Kisanga.'

'I see.'

'Also,' he said, 'you don't have to go so very far north of here before you run into cannibalism. The Kibanza practise it, so do the Kasongwa-Mule, and they're Baluba tribes. In other words you'll be in cannibal country long before you reach Katompe.'

I drew a breath and released it slowly.

'I'm not saying I'm sending you into the front line. And we serve a God of miracles, as you found out yourself last year. The point is I want you two to be fully convinced in your own minds that you are called to what will probably be a lonely and difficult job. I shan't worry if you decide against it.'

'Oh, but I — '

'And you don't have to decide on the spot. Go and talk it over with Isabel. Let it sit for a couple of days, there's no hurry.'

That night Isabel and I got on our knees and prayed until we were sure what the Lord wanted us to do. It would be a sacrifice to leave the company of other white missionaries and exchange our present living conditions for ones still more primitive, but then we had made sacrifices to come out here: it was the cost we had to accept in taking the gospel to the ends of the earth. To turn away from this, we felt, would have been a denial of the very principle of our commitment to CEM. It would have been to reject the major part of God's calling to us in the Congo, for though we couldn't have known it then, Katompe was to be the centre of our lives for the next two decades.

We told Mr Burton next morning and returned to

Kisanga to make our preparations and say our tearful goodbyes. There was a lot to pack down after fifteen months. In addition to our belongings and the inevitable souvenirs Mrs Taylor, wife of Dr Taylor who had died on furlough in Switzerland, gave me her husband's old hunting rifle and a very heavy box of cartridges — though these earned their passage by enabling me to shoot game to feed us and to barter with in the villages. In the frenzy of activity the journey's dangers sank to the back of my mind, and it was only when I had difficulty recruiting the usually enthusiastic bearers that I realized those dangers were very real. Even of those who agreed to come few wanted to stray as far north as Katompe. I remember on the third or fourth night of the trek, when we were already well into unknown territory, hearing the distant sound of drums. The fire's embers still glowed through the mosquito net we had thrown up over our beds. Isabel and I were both wide awake.

'Do you know what one of the bearers was telling me today?' she said.

'Go on.'

'About the cannibals. Apparently the bit of you they like best is the fingers.'

I stifled a laugh, and somewhere out in the starlit bush the drumming stopped. Thinking about it a second time, it was one of the least funny things I had ever heard.

Going north to Katompe you gained a good impression of how the topography changes near the Equator. Kabondo Dianda where we had disembarked from the train was near the open plains bordered in the south by the Angolan desert. Kisanga on the other hand lay in the middle of the bush: by the time you reached it the open land was liberally covered with trees, and further north these grew even thicker until you found yourself travelling with some difficulty through tropical forest. Katompe itself lay on the edge of the forest, where the trees occasionally thinned out to reveal a patch of tall grass or a marsh, depending on the lie of the land. The mission station, consisting of two small houses and a school, was planted in a concession — a plot of land granted by the Belgian authorities, for which an agreed tribute was due to the local chief. The place had been open just two years, and the only other white person living there was a South African missionary called Miss Boshoff.

It took us quite a while to get settled in. One reason for this was the unexpected proximity of the wildlife: you would often hear leopards snarling in the night, or the piercing squeal of hyenas. If hyenas were about, you could be pretty sure you'd wake up next morning missing a goat, so Dr Taylor's rifle was put to good use. Far worse than either of these, though, were the elephants. Night after night they would come around the house, trumpeting loudly and trampling on everything in sight. Since our experience in the bush fire, I had borne a sort of personal vendetta against elephants, and when they trod down the sturdy fence I had constructed to keep them out of the garden, I decided it was time I took action of a rather drastic kind. I told my headman Lupungu to wake me when he heard the elephants again.

'Bwana Lambushi! Bwana Lambushi!'

I swung my legs off the bed, parted the mosquito net and went to the window. The man's head and shoulders were outlined dimly by the stars.

'*Ngefu ya nsenga*,' he said — the Kisongye term for elephant.

In a matter of moments I was dressed and heading down the path with a loaded gun. Lupungu led the way until we arrived at the spot where he reckoned the elephants were standing. He could only guess this because under the trees the darkness was absolute and elephants, for all their enormous size, can be disconcertingly silent when they want to be. We waited around thirty seconds before we heard a familiar droning noise. I grasped Lupungu's arm and pulled him back.

'Get out of the way, it's a car!'

But I felt Lupungu's hand close over my mouth. I'd seen it was nonsensical before I'd finished speaking. There was no car on the concession, and no road capable of carrying one for twenty miles. What I had taken for an approaching motor vehicle was the sound of an elephant's digestion — working at extremely close range. The creature must have heard us because at that moment its huge bulk swung slowly out of the shadows and into a patch of leaf-mottled starlight. It was a bull — easily as large as the one that had almost trampled us near Mwanza. Pulling myself free of Lupungu's grasp I brought the rifle butt to my shoulder and let rip, then reloaded and fired again. It wasn't the wisest thing to do, firing at an elephant at nearly point-blank range in total darkness. Pandemonium broke loose. I reached for Lupungu but he was no longer there. I wondered if he'd slipped and fallen, but had no time to find out and beat a hasty retreat to the nearest large tree.

'Lupungu!' I said in an urgent whisper as the noise of the elephants grew fainter. 'Lupungu!'

A pair of pale feet lowered themselves in front of me, hung for a moment, then fell, the rest of Lupungu's body plunging swiftly after them. He landed with a thump.

'Here, Bwana Lambushi!'

We tried to follow the wounded beast for a while, but soon gave up, hampered by the darkness. At dawn Lupungu set out again with a native hunter and tracked it five miles to complete the kill. There then followed a quite extraordinary procedure. Almost the entire village moved out to camp for three days by the dead elephant, systematically cutting it up and curing it on fires, then carrying the dried strips back to the village in baskets woven from creepers. The camp itself felt like a city under siege, for we spent the nights huddled inside the ring of fires watching out for jackals and hyenas we could hear snarling in the forest. In this place a dead body was a free meal, and sitting over the smoking meat you got the distinct impression you'd jumped your place in the queue.

Finally all the work was done and we returned to the village and mission station, leaving the sparse remains to the vultures. Shooting an elephant was certainly a quick way to popularity, though I learned later that it was illegal and restricted to one beast per year even when the ban was lifted. We ate off the kill for four months, and I must say it stayed tender to the end, even though when it was still dry you needed a heavy axe to cut it.

8: *The life of a pioneer*

Katompe was a picture of CEM's work throughout the Congo. Every CEM missionary strove to build up the local church to a point where it became self-sustaining, led and taught by native Africans — strove, you might say, to make himself redundant. Very often this process of spiritual maturing would be well under way by the time he arrived, as it was at Kisanga when we took over from the Halls; but in other places it had barely begun, and there the missionary found himself stranded like a rock in a sea of paganism, not tending to churches but going out to found them. So it was at Katompe.

While Europe descended into war I roamed the Congo forests with my little group of workers, part apostle, part explorer. I was literally making my map as I went along — a service for which I ended up being twice decorated by the Belgian government. For weeks at a time we twisted and turned our way through dense jungle in a perpetual green twilight of steamy air and rotting vegetation, asking our way from village to village, receiving the primitive hospitality of the rain forest and carrying with us the precious message of salvation. We were nearly always given a hearing — a white man materialising out of the jungle was usually more than enough to arouse curiosity, and when we gathered wood and built a fire in the evening and sang gospel songs, most of the village would gather to hear what we had to say.

One curious fact about these journeys was that I was

never out of touch with Isabel. True, there often lay between us over a hundred miles of primeval forest with no telegraph, phones or radio. But as soon as night fell and the noise of the birds and insects and monkeys subsided, another sound filled the air — the drums. It's almost a commonplace that African jungles have drums beating in the middle of the night, but less often is it realised that their complex rhythms are a means of communication. The only parallel in the Western world is morse code, but I doubt if any white man could ever translate the messages that are passed from village to village, seemingly regardless of tribal conflicts, for up to a hundred miles in a single night. I could only listen to the booming of the taut skins and know that by morning Isabel would hear I was alive and well.

It was a message she needed to hear, for the sheer physical dangers of the Congo for people unused to its conditions were considerable. Not just the jungle around Katompe, but the marshlands near the major rivers and the open savanna lands to the south all had snares hidden for the unwary traveller. It was probably a sign of misplaced confidence that I decided once to head out towards Dipeba and Nzagi and take Isabel and Alan along with me. Since the wet season was almost on us it would only be a matter of weeks before all roads became impassable. The trees shook down water on us as we clambered through the forest, and we would awake in a camp wet through with dew. Still, the number of conversions the Lord gave us and the number of baptisms we were able to perform kept our spirits high, and every morning we delayed our return to get in just one more village.

Then there came a particularly heavy storm. The rain tore through the flimsy thatch of the rest house we had thrown together and drenched our beds, and we spent hours stowing our belongings under cover and searching for dry firewood. What little we found we took into another lean-to and kindled so that our bearer could start making dinner. He didn't get far; a fast flow of water was developing a few yards from the hut, and as the rain persisted this overspilled and ran over us. The fire went out, the firewood dispersed, and a good many of the articles we were frantically trying to heap on to our beds began floating away downstream.

Not surprisingly that made up our minds to head back, and after a damp night huddled in the remains of the lean-to we retrieved our luggage and made an early start homeward. The first few miles led us downhill to a small river we had crossed before by means of a rope bridge. Once over this we would be relatively safe. But when we were still a good distance off the sound of the water told me conditions had changed since we last came this way. Going a little ahead I climbed to the edge of the narrow gorge whose foliage had all but hidden the tumbling stream beneath, but had now been forced open by a roaring torrent. Half the rope bridge hung at a crazy angle above the churning brown water; of the rest the only traces were three or four creepers hanging loosely from the overhanging trees.

'We cannot cross such a river,' said the bearer whose fire had been swept away the previous night.

Isabel had caught up. 'What are we going to do, Fred?'

'We'll have to cross it, like it or not.'

'We can't go over there!'

'A man would be killed if he tried to cross,' said the bearer.

'We're doing God's work,' I said. 'The Lord will look after us.'

'Fred! Come back here!'

I pulled myself up on to the platform where the remaining half of the bridge was secured, and negotiated my way to the torn end. I was now thirty or so feet above the nearer bank of the river. The noise was deafening. I looked back at Isabel, Alan and the bearers, who wore the solemn expression of officials summoned to attend an execution. I knew Isabel would have given anything to stop me doing what I was about to do, but there was no choice, and so I dived off the broken bridge, falling several feet before I could grab the nearest free creeper. Suddenly I was swinging wildly over the water. The tree from which the far end of the bridge had been suspended came forward and backward, forward and backward. Getting control of my breath again, I used my weight to accentuate the swing until I could clutch the second creeper, transferred, crossed to a third and finally to the far bank.

'Isabel!'

I jabbed my finger at her and then beckoned. She looked around to check it was really her I wanted, and found that all of the bearers had briskly stepped back. She didn't look pleased, but I saw her gain the platform and set out across the bridge until she stood only ten yards away from me.

'Jump!'

But she shook her head.

'Jump, Isabel! It'll hold you!'

'I can't!' I heard her say, and saw her look down into the racing flood below. Suddenly she was retreating back along the bridge. 'Then get one of the bearers!' I yelled after her.

Now I was standing on the opposite bank the bearers had to follow. They came one by one, pushing the first creeper back to the next man to avoid the awful plunge I had made to grasp it. When all the bearers were over and the luggage had been broken up and manhandled across I chose the two strongest men in the party and went back for Isabel.

Cautiously she climbed out on to the bridge. One carrier stood behind her, the other hung on the far creepers; I crossed back, and by swinging hard managed to get on to the bridge with the trails of the creeper in one hand.

'Put your arms round my neck, Sweetheart.'

'Fred, I can't. I'm scared stiff.'

'You won't fall. Come along.'

With her eyes fast closed she put both arms round me and clung.

'Now push!'

The bearer on the bridge gave us a shove; we flew through the yawning gap and felt ourselves slowing for the return, but then the motion was arrested by the grip of the second bearer, and while he held the creepers together I climbed from one to the other and brought Isabel safely to the other side. That done it remained only to fetch Alan, who far from being scared jumped on my back as though he were being taken for a ride at the fair. Relieved and exhausted we all sat down and gave thanks to the Lord for delivering us. As things turned out it was more of a deliverance than we'd thought, for we heard later that the entire bridge had fallen.

But this particular journey had a kick in the tail, because when we returned footsore and weary to Katompe after weeks of travelling there was a reception awaiting us in the house. A bearer had gone in first to deposit some luggage: he came out again at a trot, wagging his head in alarm. My first thought was that our house had been invaded by *Mpaji* — red ants. The Basongye have a saying about red ants that translates something like this: 'If you see a black ant on your way, go on; but if you see a red ant, turn back.' You could add that if you see a red ant in your house, you move out, because once inside they will stay for as long as it takes them to demolish every piece of open food, which might be a whole day. There isn't a thing you can do; anyone foolish enough to disturb them will soon find them burying their heads in his arm. In fact, an old woman I knew of had been killed by an invasion of *Mpaji*, so in comparison to this the news was fairly good.

'Fleas!' I said in disbelief.

'They come in to avoid the rain,' the bearer explained, spreading a pair of pink palms and looking at the infested house. It took ten seconds to see for myself he was right — the place was literally hopping with fleas. I retreated slapping my shins.

'Well what do we do? Build another house?'

Some of the bearers giggled.

'Tomorrow we burn them out of the house.'

'But where are we going to sleep?'

We ended up sleeping in an outhouse which, though not as badly infested as the house, gave board and lodging to enough fleas for us to wake up next day scratching our ribs and looking spotty as a case of measles. When it was dry enough to burn them out our African friends bound grass together and lit it on the station fire. Brushing about from one end of the house to the other with these flaming torches they eventually swept out all the fleas, and after giving the place a good going over with disinfectant we were able to move back in.

Events like these, coming on top of what was at the best of times a difficult, hand to mouth existence, were about as much as anyone could stomach. We had seen many blessings, but after twelve months at Katompe we were so tired and longing so much to spend time with other Europeans that we decided on a whim to cycle ninety miles north to Katenta for a Christmas holiday. This necessitated the usual arrangements with a hammock and bearers, though by this time I was bright enough not to go first in line and consequently got fewer bites than usual. Three days' travel brought us to Katenta. Our arrival was greeted with uproarious enthusiasm by the missionaries, among them Leslie Wigglesworth whom we hadn't seen for a year.

'You know, Leslie,' I confided to him as I put my bike away, 'what I'm really longing for is some meat — we haven't had it for ages.'

He started to laugh. 'Well that's a thing, Fred,' he said.

'What do you mean?'

'Neither have we.'

My face must have fallen, because he added hurriedly, 'But why don't we go out early in the morning and get something for Christmas dinner tomorrow?'

'I'm on.'

But we tramped for miles through the bush without seeing a thing, which was strange considering how many animals live there. At nine o'clock we gave up and came back to the station, guns slung over our shoulders. And then I saw it — a huge white-bearded monkey sitting motionless in a tree. It was just asking to be cooked up for Christmas dinner. In an instant I had the rifle at my cheek.

'Fred . . . !'

'This one's mine, Leslie.'

I pulled the trigger; there was a blast, the gun kicked, the forest fell silent for an instant and then resumed its buzz as though nothing had happened. But the monkey had slumped backwards off the branch, and landed on the ground like a heavy sack.

'I was going to say, Fred, it's taboo to shoot that sort of monkey.'

I gazed at the bundle of white fur.

'Sorry.'

I soon began to think someone had seen us, because when we had hitched the body on a pole and were bringing it back to the station we heard loud shouts and shrieks. Laying the carcase down we ran to see what was going on. The most amazing sight greeted us: two women clutching the tail of a giant python, which was trying its best to escape into a hole in the ground. Leslie went in to help them while I reloaded the rifle.

'Pull!'

The crowd of onlookers stepped back as the snake's head snapped out of the burrow. Before it could turn I had cocked the gun and delivered two shots into the neck at close range. The creature convulsed, tossing its eight-inch tail around like a tremendous whip. When at last it lay still the villagers picked it up and carried it away. And they went off to prepare their Christmas dinner so we went off to prepare ours — or I should say, to get Isabel to prepare it, which was more easily said than done.

'I'm not going to cook *that!*'

'After we went out all morning to find it?'

'Look at it! It's practically human. Do you think I'm a cannibal?'

'You don't have to *eat* it. Leslie and I will eat it . . .'

'Then you can get the servant to cook it for you.'

'But Isabel . . .'

'He'll be used to cooking that sort of thing. I'm sure he can do it just the way they eat it in the village.'

He certainly could. During the next two hours a simply splendid aroma of roasting monkey meat pervaded the mission building. When at last we were invited to take our places at the dinner table, and we'd finished the hors d'oeuvre of watery monkey soup, I felt my stomach was about to receive the culinary treat it had been aching for since we came to Katompe. As the dish was brought in, however, something peculiar happened. One of the ladies sitting by the kitchen door got up very rapidly and hurried out of the room, and several others turned their heads away with little distraught gasps. I watched the prized monkey glide down on to the carving dish in front of me, and was instantly engulfed by a wave of pity. Sitting on the dish, naked and hairless, was something about the size of a large chicken with an oversized head laid sideways on the front of the dish.

Reluctantly I took up the carving knife. Nothing will ever erase from my memory the sight of that sad, obedient head wobbling with every thrust of the knife. It still brings tears to my eyes to think about it. Though I must say, to be scrupulously fair, once I'd detached the meat from the body and put it on my plate, and had averted my eyes from the other missionaries who were all poking their food and swallowing hard, roasted taboo monkey tasted absolutely *great*.

9: Trouble at Kongolo

The biggest problem I faced in my first tours among the Basongye was the language. Some were familiar with Kiluba, but by no means all, and so I tended to muddle along talking in a mixture of Kiluba and Kisongye, hoping against hope that I would stumble on the key to unlock the mysteries of the gospel. And mysteries they certainly were. Preaching in a completely different culture you soon discover how dependent you are on Western ideas and expressions. How for instance was I to explain the Cross and Final Judgement to people who had never seen a Roman gibbet and did not think of time as ending in a dramatic division of good from evil? In Britain a man may at least have heard of the Cross even if he doesn't believe in it, but out here you either had to explain everything from first principles — a pretty tough assignment — or find some foothold in the beliefs people already held that would help you bridge the gap in understanding.

This was what Paul did at Athens when he called his hearers' attention to a monument they themselves had raised to the Unknown God. This God, he told them, was the one of which he spoke. The Basongye didn't have an Unknown God, but they did have a number of sayings, one of which was *Mukambo ufikeile fikele ulu ba ku fikuka tui bamwagale*. It meant, literally, 'A tree propping up the sky; when it falls we shall all be spilt out', and implied that something bad was in the offing. From there it was comparatively easy to explain that the tree referred to was the special tree on which Jesus died, and that when it falls — in other words, when the time of grace is ended — judgement and disaster will follow. Similarly with the notion of resurrection. They had no word for this, but they did have a word for what happens when a man who has lain down 'dead', to allow himself to be possessed by evil spirits, gets up again 'alive', and this word — *Busangu* — provided a root for describing the Christian kind of resurrection: *Busangukilo*.

Nonetheless it was a great relief to me when after some hard work and devoted prayer I had enough converts to start a training programme for evangelists. These men would be able to preach more effectively than I simply because they knew the language and its dialects. Not only that, they would be accepted because they belonged here. They would be speaking to their own people, and eventually, with God's help, they would lead an indigenous church.

In a few months there were thirty-five men enrolled in the Bible class. As many of them were married and had children I found myself back building classrooms and houses, and felling trees to make furniture and desks. This was a strain for both of us, for Isabel was already teaching in the primary school the Omans had set up just before our arrival in 1934. Yet the school proved a valuable asset, because when the first evangelists — the *Balungudi* — were ready to take up their work, we were able to pay their wages from the sale of papyrus mats made by the school children and bought by other Europeans for floor covering.

One of the first jobs I did with the new evangelists was to visit the Provincial Government centre at Kongolo. This lay seventy miles downstream on the Congo — easy enough to reach in a fleet of dugout canoes. For a place in the African rain forest it was extremely populous: two thousand people lived in the town itself, and sixty thousand in the surrounding villages. And in the entire place there wasn't a single protestant church.

This was no accident. It was true that the remote areas were reached first by CEM, but in larger places where the Belgian colonial presence was felt more strongly the Roman Catholics had been around far longer than we had with the result that we were, so to speak, trespassing on their territory. As they had the white colonists and the administration on their side (as well as the staff of a school established by the White Fathers) this put us at a disadvantage, for far from cooperating in evangelism the Catholic priests had often been touring the nearby villages instructing people to disregard us.

Notwithstanding this I set out down river with a group of evangelists and in a short stay in Kongolo saw several conversions. The problem was, we had no time to capitalise on this. I was aware that paddling back against the current would take us twice as long as the journey down, and that when we got back a heavy building programme awaited us in preparation for the coming term's classes. If we left it too long the summer rains would come and all hope of completing construction would have to be abandoned. Wishing that we had more time available we climbed back into our canoes, promising the new converts that we'd return as soon as we could.

In fact it was to be three years before that happened. The training programme expanded so fast I was hard pressed to get away from the station, and when I finally decided to visit Kongolo again — this time with eight picked students — it was with some concern at leaving poor Isabel to hold the fort. Her health was far from robust, and responsibilities at Katompe grew daily. Sometimes I think it was only her determined will and love for God that kept her going, for her work, in which she combined the roles of mother and missionary, must have driven her to the limits of endurance. Every morning was spent taking the men's Bible class and every afternoon in looking after the wives and children. It was easier making bricks! And yet she never complained and was perfectly happy to run the mission station while I went away to preach.

As the Congo river was in flood our trip to Kongolo in 1941 had to be made over land. This was slightly shorter but a good deal less convenient because after the rains the lowlands near the town filled up with water and turned into swamps. These might be crossed by walking on logs, but in the absence of logs there was no alternative but to get in and wade. After four hundred yards waist-deep in swamp water we would emerge with our legs covered in leeches. The first time it happened I made to pull them off, but one of the evangelists warned me against it. Pull them off, he said, and you'll leave the head inside and cause an ulcer. Much better to let them have their fill of blood and fall off, for the leeches themselves hardly ever carry disease.

A worse problem confronted us when we arrived in Kongolo. We had looked out our friend who worked on the paddle steamer linking Kongolo to Bukama, and were taking our first open air meetings, when two policemen took me aside. Looking back now they were a small vision of the future: two Africans in pressed blue military uniforms and red tarbooshes. They told me to follow them to the Government office, a building I had recognised before from its white mast and limply stirring Belgian flag. Once inside, I was introduced into a large office with a correspondingly large desk, on the wall behind which there hung a portrait of King Leopold and Queen Astrid of Belgium. The man whose room it was glanced up at me. 'Sit down, please,' he said in French.

The ceiling fan whirled silently above us. I took note of the white peaked hat and the braided epaulettes: his stiff smartness reminded me of the captain on the *Llanstephan Castle*.

'Monsieur Ramsbertem,' he said at last, carefully mispronouncing my surname.

'Yes.'

'I am told that you are in charge of a mission station at Katompe that is sending native converts out to tour the villages.'

'Well, it's not — '

'Right or wrong?'

'Yes.'

'How many?'

'About fifteen so far . . .'

'So far? You intend to despatch *more* of them?'

'There's nothing to stop me,' I protested.

'And this is the reason for your arrival in Kongolo, making unauthorized speeches in the black township?'

'I've come to preach the gospel.'

'Then you can go back to Katompe and preach it there. I want you out of this town by tomorrow morning, understand?'

'Why?'

'Monsieur Ramsbertem, my country is at war. We cannot take any chances.'

'Well, my country's at war too — and we happen to be on the same side.'

'That is beside the point.'

'I'm a fully accredited missionary, working with the CEM. I have permission to be here.'

'You don't have *my* permission to be *here!*'

'Look — '

But he silenced me by slapping the palm of his hand down on the desk. Now he was shouting. 'Do you want me to throw you out of Kongolo? As Chief Administrator I order you to leave. Is that perfectly clear?'

The King and Queen gazed serenely out above his head. Suddenly the Spirit gave me an idea. 'I can't,' I said.

He glared at me.

'You represent your country, you act under orders. Well so do I. I am responsible to the CEM and to His Majesty's Government, and that means I have to respect all agreements between Britain and Belgium.'

'What are you talking about?'

'The Charter given to the Belgian Congo by King Leopold and signed by the European powers in Berlin in 1885.'

'So?'

'It allows for freedom of religion, if I remember rightly.'

'Are you trying to give me orders?'

'I'm just saying the Charter is a fact. History. I have to respect it.'

We both knew well enough who else had to respect it: I had cornered him. He stood up, bristling.

'I'll talk to you again about this.'

Taking it for a dismissal I rose and walked back to the door. When I reached it he added, in a level voice, 'All the same I swear to you that you'll never found one of your pentecostal missions here in Kongolo.'

In fact in the following weeks several churches were formed in the Kongolo area, all of them receiving the full blessing of Pentecost. Consequently I received an abrupt letter from the Administrator telling me to withdraw all fifteen evangelists from his district. He had called my bluff, for Charter or no Charter I had no power to enforce our freedom. Katenta, the other missionary centre with workers in the area, received similar instructions. Word was duly sent out to the villages for the African workers to return to their respective mission stations for prayer.

Our hands were tied. Much as we wanted to send in evangelists and great as we knew the need to be, we did not dare endanger their safety or jeopardise cooperation between the CEM and the Belgian authorities at a higher level. It was only when an old and faithful friend, Sala

Ngoi, shared with me her concern for the villages that I realised the ban did not apply to rank-and-file Christians. Sala felt God was calling her to minister in the place of the banned evangelists. I warned her that it might be dangerous to go alone, but she insisted that she was never alone when the Lord went with her, and so we gathered together to pray for her and send her on her way.

Sala Ngoi did a marvellous work in the following year. She taught from the Bible, preached the word and brought healing to the sick. Once, confronted by one of the Administrator's deputies, she made it clear the only way he could stop her from telling people what God had done for her was to cut out her tongue. It seems this made quite an impression on him, for shortly afterwards and quite out of the blue we received word that our evangelists were once again free to work in the Kongolo district. Finally the Administrator was transferred to another area and replaced by a protestant who quickly lent us his official support and permitted what his predecessor had vowed would never happen: the founding of a mission station in Kongolo itself.

10: *Every picture tells a story*

With the ban lifted I was able to make an exhaustive tour of the region round Katompe, and had only just got back when I received a summons from Mr Burton. He was still at Mwanza, 250 miles to the south. I packed my bag, kissed Isabel goodbye, and only days after returning from the tour set out again, curious to know what had made him call me in such a hurry. When I'd arrived and been given something to eat he took me round the back of his house where a large grey Chevrolet sat in the shade of a tree. I hadn't seen a car in months and it looked rather out of place here on the African plains. Mr Burton patted its front wing affectionately.

'The old lady won't start,' he said.

'Oh.' I could see something was in the offing.

'You handy with cars at all, Fred?'

I dreaded to think what would have happened if I hadn't been. Two hundred miles was a long way to come to tell someone you weren't a garage mechanic.

'You'd like me to repair it?'

'Would you?'

'Is that why you wanted me?'

'Sorry, Fred, I couldn't find anyone nearer. I need the old lady to take me on my tour of the mission stations . . .'

I smiled. 'All right. Just show me the tool kit.'

I took the car to bits, then cleaned and tested the

bits and reassembled them. Miraculously, it worked. Mr Burton drove the overhauled Chevrolet round in a slow circle and stopped beside me.

'Wonderful job, Fred, wonderful job.'

I nodded, frankly feeling pretty pleased with myself, and was just about to say 'Well, if it's all the same to you I think I'll be making a start . . .' when Mr Burton switched off the engine and said briskly, 'Good. We'll set off tomorrow.'

'Set off . . . ?'

'On tour. Wouldn't you like to come with me?'

'I was thinking of Isabel.'

'We'll send her a message. No problem.'

'How long will it take?' I said as he receded towards the house.

'Not long. Five weeks should do it.'

The trip proved very refreshing as it put me in touch with missionary friends I didn't often see. Our main destination was Kabongo, about ninety miles north-west of Mwanza, where Harold and Josephine Womersley still had their famous flying bedstead. We stayed there three days before setting out for Mutengwa, a journey that necessitated crossing the Lomani river by ferry. We were anxious to make the ferry by nightfall; missing it meant an uncomfortable night camping out on the river bank, slapping mosquitoes. At Mr Burton's insistence I set out early and by midday we'd made such good time that we decided to stop and eat under the welcome shade of a tree. It was shortly after this break that there came a tremendous thud from the underside of the car and we ground to a sudden halt.

I jumped out and wormed my way under the vehicle. I could see Mr Burton's shoes and khaki socks and his short thick shadow.

'What's up with the old lady now,Fred?'

'Propshaft.'

'Oh, I see. Is that bad?'

'Put it this way — how fast can you make a mosquito net?'

There was no reply, and presently I heard him humming.

'Can you give me that roll of wire in the boot? The universal joint's gone, but I think with wire and pliers . . .'

Half an hour later, my hands black with motor oil, I got back into the driver's seat and carefully started the engine. The repair worked — but not for long. Another five miles down the road the wire snapped and I had to get down and do the job all over again. Then again. Finally I lost count of the number of times I lay on my back reconnecting the propshaft, with Mr Burton's boots treading slow rotations as though he were watching a circling plane. With a short time left before nightfall I decided to put extra wire on the shaft in a desperate attempt to get us to the ferry. Driving as fast as the repair would allow we drew up to the crest of a hill and to my great relief and delight I saw the river below.

'Stop!' said Mr Burton.

'What's the matter?'

'Just something I have to do.'

'Can't it wait?' I cried in exasperation.

But Mr Burton was already out of the car, climbing the bank at the roadside and fumbling in his pockets. I watched in disbelief as he sat down on the grass, set up a little wooden board with paper mounted on it, and squeezed some paint from a tube. Frustration and anger seized me; here was I working my heart out to get us to the ferry on time, and what was Mr Burton doing? Sitting down to paint some ridiculous picture!

'Fred! Come up and take a look!'

Reluctantly I climbed the bank to look over his shoulder. The sun was setting over the Lomani river in a sultry blaze.

'Mr Burton,' I said, as calmly as I could, 'We are going to miss the ferry.'

'Oh, Fred, can't you see the marvellous blues and golds and purples?'

I turned on my heel. 'I'm afraid the only colour I'm seeing right now is red!' And I stomped back to the car and slammed the door.

Suddenly it gave me a sort of malicious pleasure to think we were going to miss the ferry and get bitten to death by mosquitoes. It would all be Mr Burton's fault. 'I told you so,' I heard myself saying. 'If you'd only listened to my advice . . .' But as it happened we caught the ferry and, to add insult to injury, during the eight miles that remained of our journey to Mutengwa I had to repair the propshaft another three times, now in total darkness. We were four hours reaching the mission station.

Mutengwa was blissfully calm. Next morning word was sent to the nearest trading centre, and when a new universal joint arrived three days later I was rested enough to make the repair. On the evening before we left I was sitting out on the verandah of the station when Mr Burton beckoned me.

'What is it?'

'I want you to come to my hut.'

'Is there something you want to talk about?'

But he put a finger to his lips. 'Wait and see.'

When we arrived at the little building that doubled as his bedroom and study he motioned me to go in first. Inside, set up on a table, was the painting he had started on our way to the ferry. Looking at it now I was surprised how beautiful its portrayal of the Lomami valley actually was — he had caught the blues and golds and purples just as they had been. I felt an arm around my shoulder.

'Fred, the other evening you were so tired and weary with the journey and all you had to do, that you couldn't see those lovely colours. But they were there all the time.'

The memory has always stayed with me. It always seems more than a story about pictures and ferries; even at times when we are engrossed in the darkness and difficulty of life, God's love — his sunset — is there surrounding us.

11: The black arts of the Congo

We were soon out again evangelising in the villages. But now I noticed something I'd been vaguely aware of before but had never quite put my finger on — that after the first contact with the gospel there took place a quiet stiffening resistance. People were still willing to listen, and when you'd made your point they would nod their heads in a characteristic African gesture that means, 'We understand you, go on.' But after an evening squeezed between the fire and the crowd, preaching the good news, we often sensed a reluctance to come forward and make a firm commitment to Christ. Fear was holding them back.

At last I realised it was fear of witchcraft. Of course I'd known about witchcraft since the night Teddy Hodgson had talked to us in Haslingden, but now it became suddenly and frighteningly real. In the Congo it wasn't a private fixation pursued by a few eccentric individuals: everyone was up to his neck in it. People left food outside their houses for ancestral spirits, made sacrifices to them, and built little grass huts for them to live in. They used charms and idols to ensure a successful harvest, and hired witchdoctors to protect themselves from magic and to use it against others. Most sinister of all, they formed themselves into secret societies that could terrorise an area as effectively as the Mafia.

One of our first brushes with witchcraft was against

one of these societies. An evangelist had preached in a village where one of them was operating. He had seen members of the society smear their drums with human fat and set up a tireless, angry rhythm while a witch called Madia became possessed by an evil spirit and performed a writhing dance, uttering vile, satanic things.

Only half a dozen villagers had turned out to hear him preach, but at the end he was surprised to find that one of those listening in the shadows was this witch. Of all those in the village it was she who was gripped so hard by the word of God that she could not struggle free. The demons tormented her, the drummers of the secret society pounded out their rhythms, others shouted and screamed; but though she was thrown to the ground several times by the devils possessing her, she finally turned to God and was delivered. When about a month later I came to the village myself not six but two hundred and fifty people gathered to hear the word of God, the *Myanda ibuya y'Efile*, and the following morning Madia was one of those baptised.

Battles like these were the beginnings of a war. Converts were frequently ostracised and threatened by members of their village for turning away from the time-honoured traditions of idol worship and witchcraft, and when that happened the lives even of tiny children could be in danger: no one could leave the old ways without being made to count the cost.

In a village not far from Katompe a young couple called Lewi and Alosa were converted. Just weeks after coming to the Lord they learned that Alosa was pregnant, and though this was good news it led to a struggle with unbelieving relatives, whose job it was to guide the inexperienced in the ways of the ancestors.

'This talk of the white man's Christianity is all very well,' they said to Lewi and Alosa, 'but in cases of sickness, birth or death you must go to the witchdoctor and obtain charms to ensure your safe keeping.'

The young couple called these the devil's lies. 'We are Christians,' they said, 'and we will put our trust in Jesus.'

The relatives exchanged knowing looks. When the baby was born it lived only two days.

Soon Alosa became pregnant a second time and the relatives returned, more persuasive than before. 'What happened last time will happen again if you persist in refusing the charms. This time be sensible. The missionaries will never know you have been to the witchdoctor if you wear these charms secretly, beneath your clothes.'

The couple still refused to listen. 'God will see the charms wherever we put them. No, our God will see us safely through this time. We will continue to trust him.'

The Christians prayed and the unbelievers stood back waiting for the worst to happen. They were not disappointed: soon after the birth Alosa found herself standing by a second tiny grave, murmuring through her tears, 'It is the will of God,' while the relatives said, 'We told you so!' When a third pregnancy was announced they were so sure the couple had learned their lesson that they hurried to press their advantage home.

'The witchdoctor is kind and patient and willing to overlook your past disrespect. But if you do not have the charms this time the baby *and* its mother will die.'

Alosa never faltered. 'Then I will die trusting the Lord,' she retorted.

But a harder temptation was in store, for Alosa's mother came to her hut one night with a handful of charms.

'Here, take these, and tell no one, not even your husband. I have procured them myself so that your life may be spared.'

Alosa took them, but handed them to Lewi as soon as he came home. Lewi took them back to his mother-in-law and said that, come what may, they would trust in the Lord.

The battle was on. This time the word had got round to many of the missionaries, and so countless Christians were praying, one as far away as England. Their prayers were answered with the birth of a fine baby boy whom Lewi and Alosa named Mateo. But the relatives, far from welcoming this new addition to the family, hated it with a cruel and bitter hatred, so much so that one elderly woman in the village hired a witchdoctor. She consulted him at night, and was given a small white stick. 'Whoever it is you wish to kill,' he said to her, 'must hold this stick. My deathly power will become evident within hours . . .'

By now Lewi was an evangelist-in-training and spent much of his time away at the mission station in Katompe. Consequently, although Alosa was with Mateo for most of the day there were some occasions when she could not avoid leaving him on his own, and it was when she had gone to the river to draw water that the devil made his attack through the old woman. She sat down on the ground next to Mateo and held out the stick. 'Kwata, kwata!' she said, 'Catch, catch!' Mateo chuckled with delight and grasped the stick firmly in his chubby hand.

Her mission accomplished the woman made off, but then as Mateo bashed the stick clumsily on the ground she fell over as though drunk. She picked herself up, but just as quickly went down again, and then again, as if being struck by an unseen hand. She was desperate to escape now, for many were gathering round to watch this battle of spiritual forces. It was a Christian woman of the village who plucked up courage to remove the stick from Mateo and hold it out to the woman.

'I give you back this stick you gave to Mateo that he might die by the power of the witchdoctor. You failed, for the child is well. Now I challenge you to hold one end of it while I hold the other, and we shall see whose power is the greatest — God's or the devil's!'

The terror-stricken woman flung her hands in the air.

'No, No! I dare not touch it! If I do I shall die. Your God had told me so! I do not want to die. I want to believe in your God, for what is this magic to compare with his power?' And she ran into her hut, emerging a few seconds later with an armful of charms which she flung from her before kneeling in the dust. 'Mateo's God, Alosa's God, have mercy on me!' Mateo survived to tell the tale, and the woman, putting her evil practices behind her, became known as his first convert.

If that kind of struggle took place over the conversion of ordinary villagers, you may imagine what trials were in store for the man or woman who turned to Christ from a secret society. Such a person not only denied the ways and worship of the ancestors but broke faith with a group whose secrets were too dangerous to be exposed. Thus the initiate withdrew at risk of his life.

One such person was a girl called Muloko who'd been a ringleader and devil-dancer with the notorious *Bamama* secret society. She began to attend Christian meetings and as a result of this her interest in the society gradually waned. The fact was quickly noted.

'If you become a Christian and break faith with the society,' she was warned, 'you will die — our magic will kill you.'

It was no idle threat. Muloko knew from experience that if magic proved insufficient there were a dozen tasteless poisons on hand to secure the same effect. In spite of this she decided to throw her lot in with the Christians and accept the Lord as her Saviour. Muloko was not a woman to do things by halves. The choice made, she publicly carried every charm and idol she'd kept in her little grass hut and burned them in the street. A few days later the girl who had once been the greatest obstacle to God's work in the village, and was now its greatest trophy, sealed her salvation by baptism.

The other members of the *Bamama* watched her unperturbed. 'You may have burned your charms and idols,' they said to her later, 'but remember that if you turn your back on us you will surely die.'

A few days later Muloko awoke in the stillness of the African night to find a stranger bending over her. She gave a stifled cry, sending him scurrying out into the dark, and passed the back of her hand across her lips in case he had delivered the tiny, fatal dose of poison while she slept. She found nothing, but was so unnerved that cutting wood next day in the forest she let the axe slip and embed its blade in her foot, causing a severe wound. It seemed the magic was beginning to work after all.

Suppressing her fear she went to the Christians and asked them to pray for her as she struggled to trust God in her persecution. Soon she became known as a shining example of faith in adversity, bringing encouragement to many of her fellow believers. But on top of her links with the *Bamama* Muloko had the problem of being married to an unbelieving husband who was no more impressed by her conversion than were her former accomplices in the society. Dissatisfied with her, this man decided to travel across country and find a second wife. Muloko knew that when he returned, the second wife would be the favourite and her own life, sharing this tiny hut with a second person, would be reduced to misery. None the less she committed her troubles to the Lord, and that night lay down content, not thinking that for the first time since her conversion she would be sleeping alone . . .

The next morning she was dead. Her unbelieving relatives came up to the hut to wrap her in the grass cloth used for corpses, wailing with the unmistakable 'Yo, yo yo!' that indicates a death in the Congo, and talking of dreadful visions they had seen of revenge being wreaked on the dead girl by the idols she had rejected in her conversion. The powers of darkness had done their worst.

But no one going into the hut that morning would

have thought Muloko was the victim of murder, for she lay with her head on her hand, like a child sleeping in the knowledge that its parents are near. During the night, when the stranger had stolen in with his poison, another and greater Visitor had been there to take Muloko to himself and exchange the squalor of a grass hut for streets of glory in heaven. Knowing this, the Christians honoured their sister by providing out of their scant resources a piece of real cloth to wrap her body, and at the graveside stilled the spine-chilling death wails with songs of victory.

'Away far beyond the Jordan,' they sang. 'Yes, Muloko, look out for us, for we're coming too, and if he tarries and the years dim our memory, we shall recognise you by your martyr's crown!'

12: *Two men in a boat*

As the area covered from Katompe mission station was easily as large as Yorkshire and Lancashire put together, some parts of it remained untouched for several years. This was to be explained by the terrain. One region, a stretch of the massive Congo River known as the Lualaba, ran down to the east of us between Kabalo and Kongolo. We had travelled through it on our first trip to Kongolo. Our reason for going by land the second time was that the Lualaba was in flood, making navigation extremely difficult owing to the fast flow of water and overspilling that turned low-lying areas into vast lakes.

We'd heard of forty-six villages in the area that as far as we knew had never been visited by an evangelist. We were keen to make contact with them, but the problem was finding someone to go. The backwaters of the Lualaba were a notorious breeding ground for the mosquito, and in addition anyone travelling in a dugout canoe — the only viable means of transport — faced constant danger from the hippopotamus. Most Europeans have only met the hippopotamus at a zoo, where it stands in a pool of water amiably holding its mouth open while children throw food at it. Being a herbivore it will never try to eat a human being, but if you go too near it in a canoe it'll swim out to capsize you — and that's where the real danger begins. Once you're floundering about in the water you're on the menu for the crocodiles.

I had seen the scarred limbs of men thrown overboard and mauled, and knew well enough what the dangers were. At the same time there were no excuses for holding back the gospel, and in the end I set out with no evangelists and only a small group of bearers, to do the job myself. It was tough going. I soon saw evidence of hookworm — an unpleasant parasite that enters the body through the feet and settles, with much pain to the victim, in the stomach. Not only that, but many of the villages were openly hostile. In one called Koni my bearers had to gather round to prevent me from being physically assaulted, and the noise was so great we could barely hear ourselves speak, let alone hold a meeting and address the crowd. I prayed hard as we left Koni that in his infinite power God would break down the stubborn resistance of these people. On the first trip we did see a few marvellous conversions and some of the villages actually asked us to return, but I went back to Katompe feeling that the Lualaba wasn't going to be opened up without a good deal more manpower.

I prayed for several weeks before I got a visit from Fidipa, one of my best students at the training school. He told me that God had spoken to his heart, and that he was ready to go to the river villages and preach. The news delighted me, for Fidipa came from a river village himself and understood the character of the people. We soon set off on a trip together, and after that Fidipa travelled the area several times, sometimes with me, sometimes on his own, and became a great source of blessing and inspiration. At least eight of the villages owe their conversion to him.

Fidipa was a devout man, and once when he went back to his own village he felt called to fast and intercede. After ten days of this his wife and Christian friends grew concerned for his health and wondered what it could be leading up to. They were praying with him when news arrived from the village: a woman had just died. She had been sick for some time, and her relatives, being unbelievers, had paid a famous witchdoctor to come and treat her. All in vain: he had done his evil best without effecting a cure, and had left pronouncing her dead. The wailing and crying could be heard from Fidipa's hut.

'Go and pray for that woman,' Fidipa said suddenly, to one of the Christians with him. 'She is not dead. God is going to raise her up.'

But the other man replied, 'I cannot understand this. How can I go and pray for someone who is already dead?'

Seeing he would not go alone, Fidipa got to his feet. 'Then if you will not go alone, I will go with you,' he said.

Off they went. By this time a large crowd had gathered outside the woman's hut, but Fidipa took not the slightest notice and marched right inside with the other Christian following. Falling down on his knees he began to pray for the woman to be raised up from the dead, which she was — with stunning effect. Several people were so amazed at the power of Fidipa's God that they were converted immediately, and at night, with the whole village celebrating, brought out their idols to be burned. The ten days of intercession had borne a magnificent harvest of conversions.

As time went on, other evangelists were called to follow in Fidipa's footsteps. One of them, Annanasi, went to the village of Kafumbe, which was becoming increasingly important as the war years brought first the railway linking east and west and then two transcontinental roads that crossed near the village. It was already a port of call for the river steamer on its way to Bukama, and had thus been influenced by Roman Catholicism. This early contact had resulted in a peculiar cross-breed of Christian belief and idolatry that was hostile to any sort of protestantism, which meant that the gospel had to be spread by persevering, quiet witness.

One man in Kafumbe, however, had been far more deeply affected by the gospel than any of the visiting evangelists had guessed. His name was Sefedena, a Catholic school teacher who held daily classes in the village. Since his first contact with the gospel Sefedena had been gripped so strongly by the Spirit of God that he could hardly sleep for anxiety over his sin. So when Annanasi turned up he cornered him. He knew for a fact, he said, that unless he turned from his sins he would die. They talked long into the night, and finally Sefedena made his commitment. Not long afterwards he arrived at Katompe one Sunday morning — after a walk of fifty miles — with five old men and six old women, asking to be baptised. I obliged, and they returned to Kafumbe to build themselves a mud-and-wattle church, which soon had to be replaced by a brick one because the congregation had outgrown it.

Gradually the gospel spread along the river. It even spread to places away from the Lualaba, like Kalulu, a village south of Katompe on the Kabalo border, where the fighting between villages was so fierce that on my first visit the Colonial Administration had brought the army in to quell it. There was an uneasy silence as we walked through the centre of the village and pitched our tent beneath the palm trees. We knew it wasn't going to be an easy place to preach in. It was the home of one of the most aggressive local families, in which the father and the eldest son were ringleaders of a secret society called the *Bambudye*.

In most places I visited, local villagers would help us gather firewood for the bonfire meeting, but not here. We went out on our own into the bush, and afterwards the bearers had to protect me as we went round trying to buy food. The meeting was a charade: we lit the fire, the bearers sang their songs, I preached. But although I felt we were being watched on every side, no one came.

We left the following morning, feeling as if we should

shake the dust off our feet in reproach, but we remembered the scriptural command to 'cast your bread upon the waters' and left the matter in the hands of God. Back in Katompe a few days later we were surprised to see the eldest son who led the *Bambudye* walking up our garden path. He'd been listening in the shadows when the Spirit struck him with a conviction of sin. Being given no rest, he had decided to follow us back and ask for help. I was only too glad to give it — he reminded me strongly of the eighteen year old lad who'd been brought to the Lord one Saturday night many years before in Haslingden. He handed me the tools of his witchdoctor trade, packed together in his homemade bag, and after confessing his sins and praying for forgiveness returned home to spread the good news of Jesus. Because of his position everyone had to sit up and take notice, and it wasn't long before his entire family and many of the villagers had been brought to the Lord. Consequently the atmosphere of the place changed; the old feuds died out, the fear evaporated, and the army never had to go back.

A similar transformation occurred in many of the river villages, even in the end at Koni, where one of the young bearers on my first visit felt led to return and live. He soon discovered a man who wanted to give his heart to the Lord (one I had spoken to the very first time I was there) and then revival sprang up in a wonderful way. Many were converted and baptised, and a large brick church with a corrugated iron roof was built in the middle of the village.

13: Jungle Dentist

The other part of the Katompe region that stayed closed for a long time was the extreme north where the population was exclusively Basongye. This wasn't for want of trying — I had made several trips in their country with little success, and was at my wits' end to know what to do. But then, quite extraordinarily, the Lord solved the problem.

I had come back from yet another unsuccessful tour where I had taken as my theme the text that says God is able to do exceeding abundantly above all that we ask or think. It was a little ironic in view of the gloomy mood that had taken hold of me. I felt tired and dispirited, and wasn't pleased to be woken up in the middle of my first night back home by someone coughing at the window. I got up, lit a storm lantern, and went outside.

Waiting on the doorstep was an uncommonly tall tribesman in loincloth and body paint, with bow and quiver slung over his shoulder and a spear in his hand. He made a strange and rather frightening spectacle.

I asked him what he wanted.

'You can do it,' he said.

'Er, do what?'

'You came to our villages and said you could do all things.'

'Well, look here, perhaps my language was at fault — I can do *some* things. I can't do everything.'

He looked skeptical.

'What do you want me to do, anyway?'

He opened his mouth and pointed to a large decayed molar. 'You can do it,' he repeated, looking at me with sombre eyes.

I suddenly realised he wanted me to extract the tooth.

'I can't do that!'

'But you came to our villages and said — '

'It's out of the question. Some people can do that, but I can't. Look, I'll tell you what I can do. I'll pray with you and ask the Lord to deliver you from the pain. How about that?'

He nodded, and I got him to kneel while I prayed.

'Is that better?'

He merely shook his head and repeated his conviction that I could do it.

This time I decided to obey the Word of God and anoint him with oil. When I had finished I told him to go to the village and rest until morning. But this he refused to do, threatening to remain on the verandah all night, moaning perpetually from his toothache. However he quietened down, and early in the morning I was out praying with him again.

When Isabel appeared at the door I cast a hopeless look at her.

'But Fred, you *can* do it,' she cried.

'Pardon?'

'You *can* do it!'

'What on earth do you mean — I can do it?'

'What about your pliers?'

Before I could refuse she had slipped away to sterilise them in boiling water and permanganate of potash, and presently brought them out to me in a basin. I looked at Isabel, I looked at the basin and pliers, and I looked at the man.

'Well, I'll try anything once.'

I indicated to the man that he should sit down on the step with his mouth open. Then, clamping his head under one arm, I fixed the tool's jaws on the offending tooth and proceeded to yank and twist with all my strength. With an unexpected jerk it gave way and I fell over backwards, the tooth still locked in the pliers. My patient's face broke into a broad grin. 'You have done it! You have done it!' he said, blood streaming from his mouth.

After we had both recovered I gave him strict orders not to tell anyone in the village that I had pulled a tooth. As it happened he told everyone he met, with the result that I now arrived in nearby villages to find people lining up for treatment. Fortunately, during our next trip home on furlough a dentist, who was amazed to hear the story, insisted that I show him my technique, and was kind enough to supply me with more specialised tools. I can truthfully say that those dentist's pliers worked wonders in opening the Basongye villages to the gospel.

Dentistry wasn't the only medical work we got involved in. Malaria, sleeping sickness, worms, framboesia and tuberculosis carried off young and old alike every week, and it was impossible to be true to the aims of the gospel without throwing one's weight behind the fight against them. There were a surprising number of quite simple lessons in sanitation that did a lot to prevent the spread of disease. We encouraged villagers to make beds out of bamboo instead of sleeping on the mud floors of their huts, and to replace the huts themselves with cleaner buildings made from sun-baked or kiln-baked bricks. We also tried to provide cleaner conditions for childbirth than a papyrus mat laid on the ground in the family living-quarters.

Of all diseases we came across in the Congo perhaps the most widespread was leprosy. As in other societies around the world it had dreadful repercussions, for the leper was always ostracised for fear that the disease would spread to others. Consequently many villages kept a small group of huts as a colony, and here the lepers lived, cultivating food if they were able, but otherwise completely dependent on other people's charity. Nothing could take away from them the guilt and torment of being singled out by this mysterious disease that deprived them of their friends, their social position, their livelihood and ultimately of their lives. You always knew when a leper was dying: custom demanded that he or she be taken away from the village and jammed in the fork of a tree while their huts and possessions were burned.

I remember once in the early days at Katompe, I was cycling back to the mission when I saw what looked like a bundle of clothes in the branches overhead. On closer investigation this turned out to be an old leper woman, very sick and disfigured but still alive. We improvised a seat on the back of the bicycle to take her back to Katompe, where the Christians built her a hut and my wife fed her every day until she was strong enough to walk to the school and listen at the door while Isabel taught the women. She did the same with church services, and one day I had the joy of leading her to the Lord and baptising her. I well remember her saying as she went into the water, 'You all know and see that I have got the dread disease, but it won't be long now and I shall go to be with Jesus and receive a new body!' It wasn't long, either, and I stood at her graveside feeling that if I had come to the Congo for this one soul's salvation it would all have been worthwhile.

This woman was the first member of what eventually became a large colony of lepers at Katompe. The Lord was good, and supplied all the food and clothing we required. Many of those who came were hideously disfigured, often with fingers and toes eaten away, and yet they were the most loving and grateful people I have ever worked with.

Two years after the war in Europe we were able to expand the medical work, first with a dispensary, organised by Dorothy Willis and Phyllis Ralph, and later with a small maternity unit. By the time the latter was in operation we were dealing with 400 patients a day, and every track in the forest around us seemed to lead to Katompe. We had patients from up to eighty miles away. I ought to add here that these developments were often misunderstood by some CEM supporters at home, who thought hospitals were the government's responsibility and that we were misusing resources that should have been spent on preaching the gospel. To this I can only say that medical work is an act of Christian compassion which was compelled on us then because no one else bothered. But more than that, it was a means of evangelism. It brought us in contact with an enormous number of people, and that contact was often the first step to conversion. This was particularly true of the maternity work, for to be present at a birth in this part of Africa makes you a friend for life.

A good example of the way the medical work contributed to the growth of the church is Marta's story. She was a querulous old woman, completely depressed and carried into our compound with a terrible ulcer. We had never seen one so big or so deep. But she was taken to the clinic, and while we dressed the wound we talked to her about Jesus. At first it seemed to do no good at all. She was that sad sort of elderly person for whom nothing is new, nothing is pleasant, and nothing is surprising. She seemed to have a heart of stone. We told her she should come to the meetings because they'd do her good. She came all right, but her face wore such a harsh and perpetual scowl that you needed a stout heart to carry on preaching with her staring at you. This went on for over a year, and then, suddenly, she changed. Instead of frowning she had a kind word for everyone; the ulcer that was sapping away her strength healed completely. She was baptised and found new life.

Of course there were some cases where God's own healing made the work of the medical missionaries unnecessary. Another woman with an ulcer was called Madia; hers, which began on the abdomen, grew steadily worse until her intestines protruded and finally rotted, allowing food to escape from an evil-smelling hole. In spite of this she persisted in wearing the old futile charms — feathered, crowned fetishes to which she made a daily sacrifice of chicken's blood.

There was an evangelist in her village who had often spoken to her and been rebuffed. But one day he and a group of Christian friends came over to pay her a last visit.

'Madia,' he said soberly, 'you are going to die in your sins. That is not very comforting, but none the less it is true. You get right with God and he will undertake for you. There is nothing to fear.'

She fingered the charms around her neck, and then did a surprising thing — reached up and untied them.

'You're right. It's true that my idols are lies, they have never helped me. I'll trust your Jesus instead.'

'Good. Now we'll pray for you.' said the evangelist. 'Our God can heal as well as save.'

And they prayed, at the end of which Madia added a fervent *Amen*.

In the following days the ulcer gradually healed; first the intestine closed up, and then the flesh, and finally even the tiny scar left by the ulcer vanished. There wasn't a doctor in sight.

14: Getting into print

The main effect of the European war on the Congo was a very hurried programme of road building. It never became remotely like the road-network of a western country, and very few of the roads were metalled. None the less, by the end of the forties Katompe was on a motor route, with the result that regular and tedious journeys — such as the two hundred miles I had to cycle with Alan to get him to school — could now be made by truck. It had other advantages too. One or two helpful items could be brought in that were impossible to move by hand. A generator that gave us three hours of light in the evening replaced the old oil and pressure lamps, and we were treated to the untold luxury of a long bath, filled by pumping water from the stream. We even began to get European foods.

The mission station grew. What had once been a house in a forest clearing was now a small colony. There was a church, a school, a medical centre, dormitory accommodation, a set of missionary houses — all of them built out of bricks made on site and trees hand-felled from the surrounding forest. The students changed too. Africans who before the war had come dressed in traditional clothing now wore western shorts and shirts. And there were more of them — when Isabel began teaching local villagers to read and write she had no idea that Katompe would soon have 130 boys and girls in school, plus a large number of adults and special classes for evangelists. It was only a matter of time before she needed help, and this came in the form of three qualified teachers, one European and two native African.

The bigger the school became, of course, the more necessary it was to print material for them to learn from, and eventually it was decided to obtain a printing press. We housed it in a special building, along with the paper and type. The only problem, as Mr Burton observed to me when he came up to set it in motion, was that out in the forest the machine had to be driven by foot treadles, and nobody would be volunteering to do a couple of hours' work like that in the heat of the tropics!

He agreed to rectify the situation. I don't think at that stage he had any clear idea how he was going to do it, but when he was about to set out for his next trip to South Africa he felt the Lord urging him to paint some pictures, and duly boarded the train at Elisabethville (now Lubumbashi) with a bundle of paintings under his arm. While the train was waiting he heard a commotion out in the corridor.

'Is Mr Burton on the train?' he heard a voice saying, and had barely risen to slide back the door of his compartment when an old friend arrived panting in the doorway.

'No time to explain,' he said. 'I'm leaving on the northbound train any moment. Somebody said you were here. I want some pictures.'

'What of . . . ?' said Mr Burton, untying his bundle.

'Doesn't matter,' said the other. He flipped through the contents hurriedly. 'That's terrific. I'll take the lot. How much?'

Just then the whistle blew.

'I say! I haven't got any cash! Look, take this,' he said, frantically scribbling on a cheque and handing it over, 'fill in what amount you like.' He paused only to lay a friendly hand on Mr Burton's shoulder. 'You're a pal. Must be off or I'll miss my train. 'Bye!'

Mr Burton filled in what he thought was a fair price

for his paintings and then, as the train pulled out southwards, literally sank to his knees in thanks to God. Two days later he alighted to meet another friend in Bulawayo.

'. . . and what did you say you were looking for?'

'An engine to drive a printing press. But I haven't a clue where to look,' said Mr Burton.

'I know — that is if you've got time before your train leaves again.'

Mr Burton consented, and was led to a nearby engineering works where the manager eagerly showed him a compact petrol engine complete with gearbox, wheels and belting. It was perfect, but likely far too expensive, especially in view of the cost of moving the machinery up to Katompe. Still, out of politeness he asked what the total cost would be, and it was a good job he did because it came to exactly the same amount he'd written on his cheque two days before. 'And if you want,' added the manager, 'we'll make sure it gets away on the next train.'

God moves in a mysterious way his wonders to perform. That's for certain, Mr Burton said to himself as he made the order. Soon after that the dreaded foot treadles were put away for good.

In those days a missionary's life was carried on by a constant exchange of favours and in my case it seemed every one I received left me owing about three. Not that I ever resented it. Cooperation was the only way to tackle the immense physical challenge of the Congo, and because jobs that were relatively easy in a European country — like moving a sick person to hospital — were for us at best difficult and at worst impossible, we had plenty of opportunity to find out that God is a God of miracles. Still, I have to admit it was pretty tiring, and one evening when I heard a knock on the door my first thought was 'Oh no, not another call from afar!'

Naturally it was exactly that. The African messenger

— recognisably a Basongye from the markings on his face — carried two letters in a split cane. One was from a fellow missionary, Fred Johnstone, the other from Mr Burton. Both asked if I could help in the removal of the Johnstones' belongings from Katenta to their new quarters at Kipushya. Mr Burton's reasoning was clear from his reference to an Indian friend of mine, a Hindu who had opened a small trading station a few miles from Katompe and who might be prevailed upon to lend me his old Ford truck.

In the event it wasn't quite that simple — the principle of exchanging favours had reached him, too.

'All right,' he said, 'I lend you the truck. But first you go do a trip for me down to Kabalo with a load of food.'

We struck a deal, and although we were in the wet season and the Congo was swollen I got safely over the pontoon bridge to make my delivery. When I set out the next day for Katenta I was uncomfortably aware that the rains were getting heavier and the road more soft, but I made it without mishap and loaded the truck with the Johnstones' voluminous possessions, glad to have a helping hand from Leslie Wigglesworth. On the first day of the journey to Kipushya we covered about a hundred miles before stopping at a village called Kisengwa on the Lomami river — the same river we had crossed by swinging from creepers a few years before. This was further downstream, and the river was in the worst flood known for years. A casual inspection confirmed our dilemma. The brown water was moving fast and high; it was teeming with crocodiles, and the pontoon that the ferry man employed to move vehicles across was stranded thirty yards from the shore.

We waited two days. It was a miserable wait. With no beds or mosquito nets we had to sleep together under a piece of tent canvas thrown down on the verandah of a derelict house. In an attempt to thwart the mosquitoes we tucked the canvas in tightly beneath us, only to find ourselves suffocating in the heat and taking turns to stick out our heads for a breather. Each gulp of air let in a little troupe of mosquitoes which then had to be eliminated, raising the temperature several degrees and forcing us to open up the canvas again. From the outside we must have looked like two ferrets fighting in a bag.

Two days later we were so fed up that we decided to take the risk of getting the truck on to the pontoon. We hired fifty Africans to cut down some large tree trunks which we then placed side by side parallel with the river bank. By standing the truck on two planks we were thus able to roll it out into the river. By this time we were already exhausted and driven half crazy with the flies, and we still had to transfer the truck from its makeshift platform, an operation that required raising the truck, little by little, to the same level as the pontoon. The front end came up all right, but just as I was directing the Africans to lift the rear, the back wheels slipped and we were all thrown into the water.

It was a miracle that no one was injured. With great care we lifted the back end of the truck into place, successfully raised it, and watched Leslie Wigglesworth drive it on to the pontoon. But our troubles were far from over, for it took all the strength of the African helpers, rowing and struggling frantically against the current, to prevent us being swept downstream and dashed to pieces on the rapids. To this day I firmly believe that if God hadn't been among them the worst would certainly have happened. As it was we finally scraped into the shallows at the far side, rolled the truck down and drove fifteen miles to the nearest roadside village. The conditions were simply appalling. At twelve feet the elephant grass was so tall that one of us had to ride on top of the cab to give directions, and several times the truck sank under its own weight in the soft, glutinous mud that had once been the surface of a road. After a day's work like that, without even a break for food, we weren't fussy about the quality of the accommodation (anything was better than mosquitoes and tent canvas) and it was with great joy and relief that half-way into the next day we arrived at Kipushya.

15: One people

There is a story that illustrates very well how the gospel spread in the Congo once the African evangelists had started their work.

One of them was visiting a village and had been telling a group of men the story of Jesus and his redeeming love. As the night wore on and the fire died down they left one by one to go to their beds, until only one was left — a seventeen year old boy.

'I have never heard that story before,' he said. 'I too would like to be saved.'

'All right,' said the evangelist, 'you can be saved right now.'

They knelt down together in the darkness while the boy prayed for Jesus to come into his life. When he had finished the evangelist invited him to stay longer so he could teach him more about his faith, but the boy explained that he had to leave next morning to get back to his cotton garden. This made the evangelist sad: he had seen too many young men make a commitment to God, only to forget about it in the weeks that followed their conversion. But he wished him God's blessing as they said goodbye, and their paths didn't cross again for several years.

A few months later and in a different place a missionary was preparing to leave for a tour of churches when a persistent coughing outside his door announced the arrival of a group of youths. They had walked fifty miles from their village and were asking to be baptized.

The missionary was astonished. 'Who is your teacher?' he asked.

'Oh, we have no teacher,' their spokesman replied, 'but some months ago I heard the gospel when I visited the village of Kabango. I gave my heart to the Lord that night, and came straight back to share the good news with my own people. Now these young men and myself would like to be baptised. We're not the only ones — some of the older men and women who asked Jesus into their hearts were not able to walk all this way.'

All nine were duly baptised in the river next morning. But that is not all, for as the missionary was about to set out on his journey, one of the men came running after him.

'Please — there is one thing I wish to ask you before you go.'

'Yes?' said the missionary, steeling himself for another surprise.

'The other day when I was praying in the forest I had a wonderful experience. My body was warm and tingling all over and before long I found myself speaking fluently in a language that I do not understand. Can you tell me what it was?'

He had been baptised in the Spirit. No one had prayed for it to happen, no one had even told him about it. And yet the Spirit had fallen on him exactly as it had on the first disciples, empowering him in his witness for Christ. Through an evening's fireside chat, one young man had taken the gospel home and founded a whole new church. All he needed now was Bibles and hymn books, and these the missionary gladly gave him before he went back to his village.

The gospel spread through the forest as powerfully as the bush fire in the savanna when we'd been taking Alan to the doctor. But this fire didn't leave a trail of blackened destruction behind it; you knew when it had been through a village because a group of believers started meeting together to pray and study, and sooner or later, if the village was large enough, they would build a brick church with the familiar corrugated iron roof. Over hundreds of miles members of new village churches sang the same songs and praised the same Lord. Yet as a missionary you were painfully conscious of the things that divided them: Christians in neighbouring villages belonged to communities that had hated one another for generations, raiding each other or resorting to the terrors of witchcraft. The converted cannibal might joke with missionary women, as one I know was fond of doing, by giving the flesh of their arms an appraising pinch, but for many people back in the forest such actions were in earnest.

In an effort to stamp out the old animosities we quickly got into a habit which other missionaries had begun, of holding conventions every Christmas and Easter. At these hundreds and eventually thousands of Christians — often entire families of them — gathered at Katompe to worship and learn together. Naturally this was a testing exercise in logistics. Though we sent word out by the drums when a convention was due we never knew for certain how many would be coming. In the dry season this was less of a problem because they could sleep under trees, but in the wet season a lot of preparation was needed in the construction of grass shelters. At both times, of course, people had to be fed, and it fell to me to go out into the bush a few days before a convention started and hunt for buck.

By 1954 we thought we had the whole thing down to a fine art. People poured in by their hundreds and we had days of tremendous rejoicing, from the Bible studies in the early morning to the last great gatherings around the camp fire at night. Many of the unbelievers who had been brought along were saved, and the power of the Holy Spirit was so strong that we began to feel we were in heaven itself. So a visit from the station pastor Mateo on the Thursday brought me down to earth with a bump.

'We need more meat,' he said.

'Wasn't there enough?'

'Not with these extra people. And we've got another three days to go yet. The meat will all be finished by tonight.'

I folded my arms. 'Well, I can't go out again. It's just impossible — I'm ministering two or three times every day.'

'I know,' he said. 'I wasn't asking you to. God has told me that I should go out this time.'

'Do you know where to look?'

He told me where he planned to go, saying he would leave before dawn and be back with the game by sundown at six-thirty. I agreed, and putting the matter to the back of my mind went to take the eight o'clock meeting for which a huge crowd had already gathered. After my short Bible study one after another jumped up to add his contribution to the theme, giving us a real feast of teaching. But at eleven I suddenly felt a queasy sensation in my stomach. I didn't know what had happened, but I knew with absolute certainty that Mateo was in trouble.

He had started out as he said, in the early morning, carrying with him his old muzzle-loading gun. He was scrupulous about keeping to his method of breaking branches off as he went along to leave a trail, and after four hours emerged into a clearing where he saw a couple of large antelope grazing. Knowing this would be his only chance he crept closer until he was able to lean on an old twisted tree to level the gun. But before he could pull the trigger he felt a sudden stinging pain. He looked down — there was a snake fastened to his leg. Forgetting the antelope he swiped at it with the butt of the rifle, but it was already too late: the snake was a Black Mamba — one of the deadliest in Africa. He started to retrace his steps as fast as he could, the swelling and numbness spreading through his body at alarming speed. Soon he could only walk, then stumble, and finally he collapsed on the trail.

I knew none of this. But I despatched six of our strongest men in the direction Mateo had taken and asked the people at the meeting to pray. 'Let us call on the name of the Lord to keep and watch over him,' I said, hoping the men would reach him quickly. Hours ticked by; we missed lunch, and it was four in the afternoon before we heard the men singing in the distance. I was relieved, because this familiar jogging song meant they were carrying a load, and that must mean Mateo was with them. They hurried straight up to the mission house and laid him on the verandah.

The moment I saw the swollen face and limbs I guessed what had happened, and knew also that the chances of his surviving were extremely slim. I gathered together a dozen of the older African pastors to lay hands on him. I read the passage from Acts about the cripple at the Beautiful Gate of Jerusalem whom Peter and John had raised up, then added, 'I believe that the Lord will raise Mateo up and the deadly poison will leave his body.' A great crowd had gathered round now. We cried to the Lord that he would deliver Mateo, and soon our prayers turned to weeping as we looked at the bloated body lying on the boards. Then something strange and wonderful happened. The body began to perspire; moisture trickled from the chest, pooled, and began to nose its way down and off the steps. Smaller and smaller his body shrank until we once again recognised the face of our dear Pastor Mateo.

We carried him into the visitors' room to recover. On the following Sunday he said to me, 'Bwana Lambushi, I want to go down to the church and give thanks to God and the people for saving my life. I know I should be dead by now and I want to rededicate my life to God before the whole congregation.' So we took him down to the church and he testified before a crowd so large that almost half the congregation had to stand outside, peering through the windows and trying to catch a glimpse of him.

16: *Raised from the dead*

By the following year, 1955, the missionary team at Katompe had grown to half a dozen and we were able to take a furlough in Britain. Soon afterwards we received a visit from a group of government officials — two of them in the familiar white uniform, two in suits and ties. They had come to inspect the station, and after we had shown them around they told us they were very impressed. Considering how little we had in the way of resources, they said, the scale of our accomplishments was amazing. What's more, they would make sure from now on that we received our fair share of government aid; sure enough, in the next few weeks a pair of large crates arrived packed full of medical supplies.

Then came the best news of all. In recognition of our work among the local population the Belgian government had decided to grant us a Queen Astrid Memorial Maternity Hospital. This would have a ward for twenty beds and a delivery room equipped with every modern convenience — a staggering improvement on the makeshift arrangements we had made do with up to the present. The next few months, of course, were spent building. More trees had to be felled and sawn up, thousands more bricks moulded and baked, tons of moist red soil excavated to make the foundations.

One morning I had been busy pouring concrete

blocks. I was carrying a load of gravel across to the site when I saw Isabel picking flowers in the garden.

'Lunch is on the table!' she called to me.

'I'll dump this lot and be straight back.'

She nodded and returned to the house. In the few minutes I was away some travellers arrived, and since it was always our custom to invite travellers in for a meal there were a crowd of people round the table when I got in. Isabel served the first course, but then excused herself and hurriedly left the room. I followed to find her bent double in the bathroom, being violently sick.

'What is it?'

She didn't answer.

I apologised to our guests, and after telling the kitchen help to serve the rest of the meal I put Isabel to bed and went to fetch Sister Hockley, a missionary nurse who had recently joined the station. She examined her without reaching a clear diagnosis.

'She was out in the sun this morning,' I ventured.

'Then it could be sunstroke. Not much to do, anyway, except keep her in bed for the time being, and pray she gets over it.'

Pray we certainly did, but in the next two days Isabel's vomiting and pain continued and the strange arching of her spine told us it was something far worse than sunstroke. Sister Hockley stayed with her while I went to find a doctor. This meant a fifty-mile journey to the local government post at Kabalo where, so the Africans had told me, a young Belgian doctor had just arrived. Unfortunately, the only vehicle on the station at the time was a five-ton truck, singularly unsuited to long-distance driving in the bush, but I decided to risk it and two hours later reached the Congo river, beyond which I could just make out the coloured dot that was the Belgian flag. The ferry was out of order.

After a bit of persuasion I got a couple of the ferrymen to take me over in a dugout canoe. But at the doctor's house I was to be disappointed. After I'd described the symptoms at great length and begged him to come back with me he shrugged his shoulders and said, 'I can't.'

'But she's desperately ill!'

'I can't leave the post, I'm sorry.'

I remembered the time Mr Burton had tried to get a doctor out to see Alan. I had considerably less diplomatic skill than Mr Burton. The doctor led me to the door, a firm but friendly hand on my shoulder.

'Go back straight away and bring her here. It's for the best. I have more equipment here than I can carry with me to Katompe.'

He was right. But I felt in my bones that the illness Isabel had was severe enough to make a day's travelling crucial lost time. Although it was dark I crossed the river again immediately and drove back to Katompe. As I'd suspected, Isabel had grown considerably worse in my absence. But there was nothing I could do, and in an attempt to take Sister Hockley's advice to sleep I lay fretfully awake until the first pink light of dawn. Then I went straight out to refuel the truck.

There was no possibility of moving Isabel. Every jolt seemed to send a spasm of pain through her body, making her cry out loud. Finally we decided to lift the entire mattress out of the room and lay it on the back of the truck. I think I can honestly say that the next two hours were the worst I have ever endured. I prayed continually that the old truck wouldn't give out, and yet at the same time I wished it would because with every dip in the road it pitched forward and I heard a cry of anguish from the rear. I drove most of the way with tears in my eyes.

When we reached the river we laid the mattress ever so gently on the sides of a dugout canoe and paddled across. The doctor had reserved a room for us at the local hotel and came there as soon as we were settled to start his examination. He took blood samples, then beckoned me to his side.

'Can you help me lift her, Monsieur Ramsbottom?'

'What for?'

'I need to take a sample from the spinal column.'

Isabel groaned as we pulled her up on the bed. 'Do you know what's wrong with her?' I asked.

If the doctor had had any doubts they were dispelled the moment he pressed the needle into her spine. Fluid shot like a fountain across the room.

'Meningitis,' he said.

For eight days he fought to control the sickness with lumbar injections. The injections themselves were harrowing in the extreme as they required Isabel to be moved into a seated posture with her back straightened against the forced and painful arch. On the eighth day it took three strong men to hold her in position. By this time I had sent messages to Katompe and to the Womersleys at Kamina asking for their prayers, but Isabel only seemed to get worse under the combined strain of the sickness and its treatment. Close on ten o'clock that night as I sat beside the bed I saw a drastic change come over her. She gave the slightest twitch, and suddenly her eyes fell half open. I knew instinctively that she had suffered a major stroke.

The doctor came immediately. He stayed with her for over an hour before turning away and putting his arm gently round my shoulder.

'I'm afraid she's gone.'

I stood silently for those few seconds nearly all of us experience when someone's life has finished and yet we're still here, alive. The doctor was saying, 'I'm sorry, but I'll have to go and find another room to put the body in. Then it will be necessary for you to go to the Administrator to get some boards for a coffin. . . .'

'No.'

'Monsieur Ramsbottom — ' he urged gently.

'No,' I said, my voice thick with emotion, 'I still believe God can raise her up again, even now.'

The doctor hesitated and threw a glance at Sister Hockley, but before he could say anything I had pushed between them, and was out of the room.

'I'll be down at the river,' I called back.

For once oblivious of the mosquitoes I sat down by the Congo river, alone in the darkness with the Creator. The lapping of the unseen water was obscurely comforting: it made me think of the first chapter of Genesis: 'The earth was without form and void, and darkness was upon the face of the deep . . .' The Spirit had moved on the waters, brought light out of darkness, order out of chaos. And I knew he was going to do it again, here in the Congo. The Great I AM was going to show once again that he was the same God who led the Israelites through the Red Sea and brought Jesus back from the dead, the same yesterday, today and forever. Suddenly across the water there came a bright shining light that momentarily enveloped me in its radiance.

I jumped up and ran back to the hotel, and opened the door of the little room to find Sister Hockley in tears.

'Fred! I just saw the Lord. He walked in at the door, went to the head of the bed, stretched out his hand and breathed on Isabel and said "Live!" '

I approached the bed and took Isabel's hand: it was warm, her cheeks pink. She was breathing normally.

She was alive again.

'Glory to God!' said Sister Hockley.

It was then that the door opened and the doctor came in, a pair of Africans behind him with a stretcher and a blanket. He entered in discreet silence, drew level with us at the bedside, and saw the miracle. He may have been a Catholic, I don't know; but his first words when he saw Isabel were, 'God has been here.' He knew Isabel had been dead, and he also knew who the one Person was who could raise the dead to life.

Next day we were joined by Harold and Josephine Womersley, Horace Butler and Walter Hawkins, who had travelled five hundred miles over treacherous roads to be with us at this hour of need. I was grateful beyond measure — it was over two weeks since I had got a good night's sleep — besides which Isabel still had a long way to go before she regained full health. For the first few weeks she could move only her eyes — the rest of her body was paralysed. None the less the doctor declared that the God who had brought her back from death would surely complete the healing work. So when the other missionaries had returned to their stations we carried Isabel out again on her mattress and drove back to Katompe. This time, mercifully, there were no cries of pain.

At first we had to take it in turns to feed her, massaging her throat to help her swallow. But gradually she improved and was able to eat a little solid food. Then she grew strong enough for us to lift her from the bed during the day and carry her into the sitting room. Finally, much to my delight, she said to me, 'Fred, make me a stick. I'm going to walk again!' In no time at all I had fashioned a stick from rosewood and polished it until it shone, and the next day, with the stick on one side and me on the other, Isabel took her first steps since the day the meningitis attacked her. It wasn't easy at first. But her indomitable will and gritty determination again won out, and in a few months, by the grace of God, she was walking normally. For someone who'd been dead I thought that was absolutely marvellous. How great is the God we adore!

17: Out of the Congo

New mission stations had now been opened not only at Kongolo, but also at Katea, Kashiukulu, Albertville, Kabalo and Nyunzu. Hundreds of new churches had been built, and with the help of the local evangelists the enormous area surrounding Katompe had been thoroughly evangelised. But by our Easter convention of 1957 change of a different sort was in the air. That year our speaker was my old friend Leslie Wigglesworth. In the course of our conversation one morning he mentioned some new government training programmes.

'I'd never heard about those' I said.

'Crash courses, they call them. The Belgians are in a hurry to train up native professionals.'

'Why?'

'Exactly what I wondered. But when you think about it, it isn't that hard to put two and two together. India, Pakistan and Ghana just last month.'

'Independence!'

'We've seen one or two little signs of unrest. It's like a snowball. Once it starts rolling it gets bigger and bigger. The Belgians seem to know which way the wind's blowing.'

'When's it going to happen?'

'Who knows? I don't suppose the government would ditch the dominion unless it was forced to, and they aren't going around publicising dates. I suspect they're under pressure.'

'Pressure from whom?'

'Ever heard of a man called Lumumba?'

'No.'

'He was thrown out of two missionary schools — one Catholic, one Presbyterian. He was in the Post Office service for a while. Now he's in politics.'

'And he's leading a movement for independence?'

'That's the rumour — and I do know that Lumumba has an uncanny ability to make tribes settle their differences.' Leslie tossed a glance at the crowd of visitors to the convention. 'The gospel's not the only thing that breaks down tribal feuds nowadays. Fear and hatred of a common enemy unites people just as well as love.'

In the isolated world of African forest, far away from the struggles of the rest of the world, the word 'enemy' had ceased to have much meaning for me.

'Think about it,' said Leslie. 'To the African the white man may bring medicine and tools, but he's also the boss. The highest rank an African can reach in the army is Sergeant-major — all the officers are white. The white man has run the country, given the orders, made the rules, ever since he came. And that goes for us, too.'

'But we're trying to make the church self-sufficient.'

'I'm just saying it may not look that way from the outside. And even if it does, whose church is it, anyway? Jesus was Jewish, but to them he'd be another white.'

We joined the meeting. It was a marvellous time of worship; as so often happened, many of the unbelievers who had been caught up in the throng of the convention raised their hands for salvation at the close of Leslie's address, and many believers came forward to make a fresh commitment to their Lord. So strong was the presence of God among us that only with great difficulty could the meeting be closed. There was a short break before the second gathering, this one led by some native evangelists. They expounded the text, 'One faith, one Lord, one baptism' with such power that the listeners' hearts were moved and their eyes filled with tears. From this we went on to a Bible study. The questions came fast and earnest, and it was only with the help of the Holy Spirit that we were able to answer them. Noting the sea of eager faces and the scratching of pencils on notebooks, I acknowledged it was miraculous that these men, who a few short years before could neither read nor write and were buried in the darkness of idol worship, were now able ministers in the service of Christ. Together they made up the network of local church leadership that had penetrated the deepest forests of the Congo. And yet it was a network of which we, the white missionaries, were still the centre, and the Africans the dependent fringe. If we no longer did the frontier evangelism ourselves it was because we directed them to go and do the job for us.

The final hours of the day were given over to testimonies. One among the first to stand up and speak was an evangelist called Yakoba, who told us he had endured much difficulty on account of a man in his village who even in the grip of paralysis cursed God and called upon his charms to deliver him. The condition had slowly worsened until one night, totally immobilised he heard God speaking: 'You must send for those whom you have cursed and ridiculed.'

When he recounted this to the other villagers next morning they laughed him to scorn, but he gave them no peace until one agreed to fetch Yakoba as the Lord had dictated. The evangelist arrived with a small group of Christians, and putting behind him all the things of the past went in like the Israelites to possess what lay ahead. The paralytic was lying in his hut. Yakoba was surprised to hear him apologise for all his past misdeeds, and duly prayed that God would save and heal even this old rebel. Hardly had the words left his mouth when the glory of God came down and the man was instantly healed. In a few days he had repented not only before Yakoba but before God, and had become a Christian.

As Yakoba sat down, another evangelist, Palodo, sprang to his feet. 'A while ago my village was invaded by tsetse fly . . .'

The crowd nodded in the distinctive African way: they all knew that sting like the touch of a hot poker, and the sleeping sickness it brought. In this case, Polodo went on, the mind of the local Christian teacher had been strangely affected by the disease. This greatly pleased the witchdoctors. 'This is what comes of believing in the white man's god,' they said.

A short time later the disease claimed its second victim — another Christian. The people of the village danced and sang until they were beside themselves. Their charms, they said, had protected them from the disease — more than the white man's god was doing, for the sick woman was deteriorating by the hour. Anxious relatives decided to call in witchdoctors in the hope of casting out what they call the 'white devils', but neither their magic nor the prayers of the Christians could arrest the illness, and the woman eventually lost consciousness and died.

This was the signal for a grisly wailing to begin. Even as the relatives emerged from the hut to set about finding a shroud and digging a grave, Polodo and his friends still persevered in prayer, and shortly before the burial they received a witness that God was going to act in a miraculous way. They hurried along towards the mourners. No sooner had they appeared than the relatives cursed and called down afflictions on them, but they resolutely walked into the hut where the body was wrapped in its shroud, and began to pray. While the wailing continued outside the corpse twitched, then grew warm, then started to breathe. The woman they were just about to bury had come back to life!

'Praise God!' said Paloda to the listening crowd, and was answered by a chorus of praise. Through the telling of his story we had all sensed a strengthening of the presence of the Holy Spirit in our midst, and now that

Polodo had finished the spontaneous outbreak of thanksgiving died away into an expectant hush. We might have been gathered at the foot of the Cross, so intense was the sense of God's nearness. Then in the silence an evangelist called Kabila Dibala rose to his feet.

'We have been working for the Lord at Katompe for many years,' he said. 'The Lord Jesus brought Mukelenge Lambushi and Madamo Lambushi from a far country to tell us the good news. They gave up everything to come here, and because they came we have heard the gospel. Now we are privileged to help in preaching the word of God. But I remember that the Apostle Paul said, "I will not be burdensome to you; for I seek not yours, but you . . . " Paul was not paid to preach the gospel, nor were our missionary brothers paid to preach it. Then I ask myself how I can allow myself to be paid. I hear the voice of God calling me to step out in faith. I shall take nothing more in exchange for my work. I shall go out in faith, trusting him to provide . . .'

The next day when Kabila Dibala and another evangelist brought their gifts to the church, they refused to take anything as salary. They had the joy of the Lord in their faces as they set out to preach Christ to their villages, and it wasn't long before a further thirteen followed their example. I was delighted. This moment — one I had been working towards in Katompe with my wife and fellow helpers for over twenty years — had arrived when I least expected it and most feared for the future of the Congolese church. And in fact the Spirit moved in the same way throughout the Congo, for in 1959 CEM was able to hand over official control of the church to its indigenous leaders.

It came in the nick of time. Over the next three years the distant rumours of unrest took on the solid form of political events. Lumumba's influence grew as he went around whipping up support. The promises he made were wild and inflammatory — when Independence came, he said, people would no longer have to drive on the right side of the road, and every black man would be able to take a white woman as a wife (hardly likely as whites had always been outnumbered by at least ten to one) — none the less his uncompromising demands for loyalty to himself and his Soviet backers won over huge sections of the African population. At Kongolo, where there was a military camp, only the intervention of a padre prevented insurrection with slaughter of the white officers. Finally the Belgian government set a date for Independence.

As the crucial year arrived I was beginning to feel the effects of my long stint in the tropical climate. The bouts of malaria that quinine had never quite held at bay had weakened me considerably, and now in addition I was suffering from an attack of the parasite known as filaria loa. When it became evident that I couldn't carry on much longer, arrangements were made for a long and much needed convalescence in Britain, and in May of 1960 Isabel and I packed our bags and caught the plane home.

On June 30th the Belgian Congo became the Congo Republic with Patrice Lumumba as Prime Minister. Seven days later the army mutinied, and in the chaos that followed much of the region we had evangelised was overrun by rebel forces. Two CEM missionaries were killed; many of the rest were evacuated, leaving only one out of thirteen stations run by white missionaries. At Kongolo, the stronghold of Catholicism, eighteen priests were murdered and thrown into the Congo river. What was happening to the African Christians we knew and loved we could only guess at.

18: Back to Zaire

Then the letters began to arrive. These accounts of the civil war and persecution, often first-hand, were sickening to us. While Isabel and I went around on deputation work in Britain our brothers and sisters were being killed for their faith because they had learned it from the white man. Mission houses were being plundered, churches burned down, villages abandoned, people turned overnight into refugees. Their suffering weighed so heavily on my mind that it was almost a relief to be summoned by the Home Director. He introduced me to a lean, tall man with dark hair and a handshake like the grip of a vice.

'This is Bill Dalby.'

'Pleased t'meet you.' He had a strong Glaswegian accent.

The Home Director invited us to sit, and went on, 'I asked you here, Fred, because I think there may be a chance of getting back into the Field. Bill here spent a couple of years in Eastern Kasai before Independence, but we'd also like to send in someone with more experience of the country. I wanted to sound you out about going back in, just the two of you.'

'I'd go tomorrow,' I said.

He nodded. 'I knew you'd say that. But I must warn you of the dangers. The political situation's still very unstable. You might be sent back. You might not get in at all. Either way it'll mean leaving your families behind until it's safe.'

'Will we be going to Katompe?'

'Not as far as that. We're aiming at Bill's old stamping ground in Kipushya. And you won't be able to get there by the south, either. The only way into the interior for a European at the moment is via the capital, Kinshasa. You'll appreciate that once you get there the situation will be very much in your own hands. We can't book your passage any further than the Belgian airline.'

The very thought of returning to the Congo was a tonic to me. In a matter of weeks we had prepared for our journey, and said goodbye to our wives before flying to Belgium and catching the plane south. Like my trip many years before on the *Llanstephan Castle* it was relaxing and uneventful. Not so once we reached Kinshasa: we soon learned that Lumumba had resolved his difficulties by calling on the United Nations Security Council, with the result that the capital now had a strong presence of UN troops. Every new arrival in the country was suspected of being a mercenary, all the more if they showed an interest — as we did — in going into the bush. Consequently three days of negotiation with local officials got us absolutely nowhere. Not that they were rude or offensive, but as one of them put it, 'We would be completely unable to guarantee your safety on such a trip, and so we cannot issue you with visas.'

'I can only suggest,' he added as an afterthought, 'that you go and see the Minister of the Interior.'

'What's his name?'

'Jason Sendwe,' the man replied, with a look on his face that suggested it would surprise him greatly if we got within a mile of the Minister's office. But as it happened the name was very familiar, and after a lot of perseverance with the guards at the Old Belgian government offices we were shown into a palatial room in which a black man in a three-piece suit sat behind a monstrous desk. He jumped to his feet as soon as he saw us.

'Bwana Lambushi?'

'Jason Sendwe!'

We grasped each other's hands, then I introduced Bill and we sat down. 'I met you at Kabongo,' I said.

'I remember.'

'I was there when Brother Womerley baptised you!'

'That's *right!*' said Jason, slapping his hand on the desk.

After that we passed several minutes exchanging reminiscences, before coming on to the present trouble.

'What happened to Mr Lumumba?' I asked.

'Lumumba is dead.'

'I heard he had been dismissed after civil war broke out.'

'Yes. He appealed to the United Nations for protection but Colonel Mobutu captured him and sent him to Katanga, the province that tried to break away in the civil war.'

'And he was executed?'

'Who knows, Brother Lambushi? It is enough to say that he died in mysterious circumstances.'

'Who's in charge of Katanga?'

'A man called Moise Tshombe.'

That name too was familiar. I remarked to Bill, 'It's as if all the old boys from the mission schools are now running the country.'

'And what are you doing back here again?' asked Jason.

We explained our objective of getting across to Kipushya.

'That will be very difficult. Everyone is a suspect, even if he has the right papers.'

'Can you help us to get papers?'

'I will do all that I can, Brother Lambushi.'

He called in an assistant who left the room in a hurry and returned a while later with printed sheets in his hand. Jason Sendwe looked them over, signed them, and gave them to us. 'And now, before you go, Brother

Lambushi, will you say a word of prayer?' We prayed for him, thanked him profusely, and left the office little knowing that would be our last meeting. Shortly afterwards he was killed by rebels on a visit to Albertville.

He had chosen his words carefully in saying he'd do what he could, for although we would never have left Kinshasa without the papers they didn't save us from being held up and questioned on the journey. We were delayed for two days without food or beds at the air terminal before we managed to see the Commandant of the UN, and when we had explained that we wanted to go a thousand miles east he told us flatly there were no civilian planes going in that direction.

'Is there nothing at all?'

'The UN do have cargo planes heading out that way . . .' He looked at us thoughtfully. 'You said you were going out for mission and relief work? Well, I think we could justify that. But it will be a very uncomfortable journey. Excuse me while I check the schedule.'

He got up and left the room, and Bill and I prayed earnestly that there would be a plane. There was one, due to leave in half an hour; in a matter of minutes we were out on the runway watching 40-gallon drums of aviation fuel being loaded on to a Dakota. The commandant was right about the quality of accommodation. Six hundred miles locked in a confined space with fuel drums almost asphyxiated us, but we made it, and arrived in a town neither of us had visited before, called Luluabourg.

The peculiar thing about this place was that it looked almost completely deserted, and yet gave you the impression you were under constant surveillance. We walked warily along the main street and eventually found an old trader who was willing to put us up until we could find a means of covering the remaining four hundred miles of the journey. It didn't entirely surprise us when shortly after our arrival four fully-armed soldiers came and took us off to the town commandant. Once again we were made to rehearse our reasons for travelling to the interior and once again our papers were scrutinised. Finally, after several days of detention and without a word of explanation or apology, we were released.

In the meantime our friend the trader had been making enquiries for us. He had found a Belgian — one of the few remaining in the country — who had a plane and was willing to fly us to Kabinda. All we had to do was turn up early next morning at the airstrip. This we did, in the middle of a rainstorm, which proved providential because it prevented anyone else from seeing what we were doing. The Belgian led us to the hangar, casting appraising glances at the sky.

'We'll have to wait until the ceiling lifts,' he said.

It sounded slightly comical to be waiting for the ceiling to lift — as though we were going to take off from inside a house. Half an hour passed while the sun rose, bringing full daylight. We listened for the sound of footsteps, but none came. I told the Belgian that it was kind of him to risk his plane on us, but he replied only that Europeans had to stick together when times were hard and that he certainly wouldn't accept anything from us in excess of his fuel costs. Shortly after that the ceiling lifted and we took off.

It was several hours later that he pointed over the side to a smooth patch shaved off the dark green jungle. 'That's Kabinda. It's as near as I can get you. Now listen. When we get down I'm going to turn straight round and go back. I won't shut off the engine. For a start there's no knowing what they've got down there, and if it's machine guns I want to be out of the way as soon as possible. I don't want this plane shot up or impounded.' We nodded, and the plane made its descent, bumping down on the runway. When it had slowed to a walking pace Bill flung open the door and tossed our luggage out. We jumped. The pilot shouted something like, 'Good luck!' and accelerated away.

The first thing we noticed was the silence; the second, which came almost immediately, a crowd of Africans running at us on every side brandishing guns and machetes. My heart gave an involuntary flutter. I was almost sure there would be men among them who would recognise me, but it was only when one got within twenty yards that he shouted out, 'Bwana Lambushi!'

We were given a tumultuous welcome, and made the two-mile journey to the town singing all the way. We stayed for two days before someone from Kipushya turned up on an errand with an old truck. He was so overjoyed that he completely forgot what he'd come for and took us on board instead. The truck wheezed and gave out a few miles short of a town with a cotton factory, but we didn't mind walking the rest of the way. We met up with the Christians there, and about noon the next day heard the truck catching us up to cover the last twenty miles to Kipushya. We came to a carnival atmosphere, for a crowd of men and women and children ran out to escort us in. Anyone watching would have thought Bill and I had liberated the country single-handed.

19: The last chapter?

The first thing we noticed on our arrival in Kipushya was the suffering caused by civil war. The joyful eyes that welcomed us were sunken in their sockets, and the children's bellies bloated for want of nourishment. Food and clothing were in short supply; malaria, worms, parasitic diseases, TB, leprosy and anaemia were all rampant for lack of medicines to treat them. Not only that, but so far away from the capital law and order were on the verge of breakdown. You could hardly move without hitting a roadblock where as often as not the soldiers were drunk, inquisitive, and, if you were driving a car, chiefly interested in getting their hands on the keys. Every day delegations arrived at the dilapidated mission station we had made our headquarters, asking us to visit distant villages. We went to a few, and found the same depressing situation in all of them; it wasn't possible to cover them all. After three months of reconnoitring we decided it was best to return to Britain and see what support we could enlist over there. We made our way back to Kinshasa, and after obtaining papers for our return, caught the plane to Europe.

Our tour in Britain was extremely successful, for God gave us plenty of opportunity to report on what we had seen. For our second trip CEM selected a number of extra missionaries to go with us, and as a result of an unexpected interview with Oxfam we were allocated a large sum of money for relief work and promised medical assistance, food and blankets as soon as they could be sent out. When we got back to Africa we set about rebuilding the mission station and its medical facilities. It wasn't long before the sick were once again receiving adequate treatment and people who had been reduced to wearing rags were dressed in an assortment of second-hand western clothes.

At first our mobility was severely restricted simply because we lacked any means of transport to outlying areas. But one of the first consignments from Oxfam included a forward-control Land Rover, and very soon I was driving to as many of the surrounding villages as I could find, bringing supplies of food and clothing. It was a shock to discover many of them abandoned, the buildings in disrepair, sometimes showing evidence of violent destruction. Often all that remained of a church I had seen erected in the years before Independence was an empty, roofless shell in the centre of the village site. Visiting one north of Kipushya I got out of the Land Rover and looked inside: among the buckled sheets of corrugated iron and the burned-out crossbeams lay a pile of white bones, the remains of perhaps fifteen or twenty people who had been Christians, maybe evangelists and pastors in that area. I wondered if I had known them — almost certainly I had.

On first inspection it appeared that civil war and persecution had undone years of painstaking labour, but this was not so. On the contrary, the places of most savage persecution were those where the light of the gospel now burned most brightly. As the Roman rulers discovered in ancient times, persecuted Christians multiply fast. Consequently when what they called the 'troubles' began to abate, a fire of revival swept through the area. Mighty miracles were performed, men and women converted in their thousands, churches rebuilt larger than they had ever been before.

By the end of the sixties the area of the evangelistic work begun by CEM (now called the ZEM — Zaire

Evangelistic Mission) had grown by a factor of four. Even the apparent setbacks, when fighting broke out and we had to be evacuated, ultimately served the purposes of the gospel. The arrival of the Mulele rebels from the north precipitated a very hurried departure to the diamond-mining town of Mbuji Mayi. A couple of missionary friends flew in to collect the women while I drove the men away in a truck. It was two months before a reconnaissance flight in a light plane convinced us the region was clear, and by that time the pentecostal message had started to flourish in Mbuji Mayi. (Incidentally the airfield at Kipushya was another product of the period — a thousand yard strip of land cleared by hand and smoothed over with sand.)

The old convention meetings were revived, but so many people now came that it was necessary to put up a huge shelter of palm fronds to protect them from the sun. I remember at one of the last conventions I attended a local preacher spoke on Acts chapter 3. He quoted the words of Peter, 'Silver and gold have I none, but such as I have give I thee: in the name of Jesus Christ of Nazareth rise up and walk.' He didn't know that listening to him in the congregation was a young man who'd been lame since birth and could only drag himself along with two wooden blocks in his hands, so that the skin on his knees had turned as tough as animal hide. Before the preacher had even finished his message this man began pushing and shoving his way through the crowd. When he at last made it to the front he cried out to the elders for deliverance. They didn't hesitate to pray, but before they had laid a hand on him the Lord had already acted, for he started pulling himself up on the arms of some bystanders. Suddenly he was swaying on his feet, and then, as the power of God surged through him, he began to walk. With exclamations of excitement the crowd parted before him. The miracle had yet to be completed, for as soon as they saw him healed two other cripples in the crowd climbed to their feet and walked. The congregation rose as one man, arms raised, praising God with heart and voice.

It struck me I was watching a re-enactment of something that happened at the very start of the church's life. That healing, of which the preacher had spoken, had carried the Spirit of Pentecost into a miraculous ministry. And now here it was happening all over again in the middle of Africa! Not that many wonderful things hadn't happened already — they certainly had — but now those seemed only a preparation, a sowing and watering of the seed. Isabel and I had watched in wonder as God gave the growth. We had started a work in my home town of Haslingden, helping to plant one new Assembly. Here after a lifetime in Central Africa we can point to no fewer than four thousand Assemblies which God has raised up in the ZEM alone.

Pondering that we can only exclaim 'See what God has done!' Hallelujah!

Other Marshall Pickering Paperbacks

FORGIVE AND RESTORE

Don Baker

When a member of God's family, in this case a loved pastor, goes seriously off the rails in his personal life, the questions looms large, What should the church do about it? Is it a matter for the church leadership only? Should the wayward member be asked to leave or just relieved of responsibility? What should the congregation be told?

This book is a remarkable account of how one church dealt with such a highly charged and emotional crisis. It records in honest detail the ebb and flow of hope and despair, uncertainty and humanity, and relying throughout on biblical principles, it picks its way through a tangled mess to find a place of healing and restoration again.

WHEN YOU PRAY

Reginald East

Spiritual renewal has awakened in many Christians a deeper longing to know God more intimately. Prayer is the place where we personally meet God, yet it is often treated simply as the means for making requests for our needs, and offering our stilted, dutiful thanks. In this practical guide to prayer, Reginald East shows how we can establish a prayer relationship with God which is both spiritually and emotionally satisfying. Through understanding God and ourselves better, prayer can truly become an encounter with God, where we relax into Him, enjoy Him, listen as well as talk to Him and adventure into discovering His heart of love.

If you wish to receive *regular information* about *new books*, please send your name and address to:

London Bible Warehouse
PO Box 123
Basingstoke
Hants RG23 7NL

Name ______________________________

Address ______________________________

____

____

____

I am especially interested in:

- ☐ Biographies
- ☐ Fiction
- ☐ Christian living
- ☐ Issue related books
- ☐ Academic books
- ☐ Bible study aids
- ☐ Children's books
- ☐ Music
- ☐ Other subjects